The OPTIMISM MINDSET Bible

Master the Law of Attraction

Manifesting

Love | Wealth | Abundance | Success | Money.

Power of 369 Method.

Positive Psychology ● Hypnosis ● Affirmations.

YOUR MIND CREATES.

Mark Allen

© **Copyright 2023 - All rights reserved.**

The content contained within this book may not be reproduced, duplicated or transmitted without direct written permission from the author or the publisher.

Under no circumstances will any blame or legal responsibility be held against the publisher, or author, for any damages, reparation, or monetary loss due to the information contained within this book, either directly or indirectly.

Legal Notice:

This book is copyright protected. It is only for personal use. You cannot amend, distribute, sell, use, quote or paraphrase any part, or the content within this book, without the consent of the author or publisher.

Disclaimer Notice:

Please note the information contained within this document is for educational and entertainment purposes only. All effort has been executed to present accurate, up to date, reliable, complete information. No warranties of any kind are declared or implied. Readers acknowledge that the author is not engaged in the rendering of legal, financial, medical or professional advice. The content within this book has been derived from various sources. Please consult a licensed professional before attempting any techniques outlined in this book.

By reading this document, the reader agrees that under no circumstances is the author responsible for any losses, direct or indirect, that are incurred as a result of the use of the information contained within this document, including, but not limited to, errors, omissions, or inaccuracies.

CONTENTS

INTRODUCTION 1

CHAPTER 1: MASTERING THE LAW OF ATTRACTION 5
   What is The Law of Attraction? 7
      How Does it Work? 8
      What Can I Achieve with the Law of Attraction 9

CHAPTER 2: MANIFESTING LOVE 13
   How Can You Manifest Love? 15
      Practicing Self-Love 17
      Getting Clarity and Shadow Work 19
      Manifesting Love With Positive Self-Talk 23
      The Power of Visualization 31
      Believing and Embodying 38
      Taking Action 43
      Sustaining Manifestation 45

CHAPTER 3: MANIFESTING WEALTH 49
   Why Getting Comfortable With Spending Money is Important 54
      Putting Yourself Into Abundant Environments 57
      Visualizing Wealth 59
      Goal Setting 61
      Budgeting For Manifesting Wealth 66

CHAPTER 4: MANIFESTING ABUNDANCE 69
   Your Beliefs and Your Desires 70
      Effort and Positive Emotional States 75
      Process and Perseverance 78
      Why Hypnosis Works 80
      The Importance of Patience 82

CHAPTER 5: MANIFESTING SUCCESS 85
   Goal Setting Once More 88
      Visualization Techniques for Success 92
      Meditation for Success 95
      Failure and Mistakes 98
      Internal vs. External Motivation 101

CHAPTER 6: MANIFESTING MONEY 109
   Acknowledging Your Past 110

- Setting Financial Intentions 114
- Taking Risks and Facing Your Fears 118
- Mimicking Others 122
- Genuine Charity 124
- Investing in Yourself and in Your Team 127
- Enjoying What You Earn 132

CHAPTER 7: THE 369 METHOD 135
How Does it Work? 138

CHAPTER 8: POSITIVE PSYCHOLOGY 143
What is Positive Psychology? 145
- The Building Blocks of Well-Being 153
- Benefits of Positive Psychology 154
- How to Be More Positive 159

CHAPTER 9: HYPNOSIS 161
How Hypnotherapy Works 167
- Benefits of Hypnosis 168
- Hypnosis Method 1: Conscious Breathing 170
- Hypnosis Method 2: Guided Visualization 173
- Hypnosis Method 3: Positive Suggestions 175
- Hypnosis Method 4: Regressive Counting 176
- Hypnosis Method 5: Relaxation Anchors 177
- Hypnosis Method 6: Guided Self-Hypnosis 178
- Hypnosis and Positive Psychology 179

CHAPTER 10: AFFIRMATIONS 183
Your Brain on Affirmations 186
- A Quick Note on Self-Identity Theory 189
- Taking Advantage of Your Mind's Laziness 190
- Affirmations and Beliefs 193
- Ways to Incorporate Affirmations Into Your Life . 198

CONCLUSION: YOUR MIND CREATES 201

AFFIRMATIONS 207
- 200 Affirmations on Couple Love 207
- 200 Love Affirmations for Single People 210
- 200 Affirmations to Attract Wealth and Abundance . 214
- 200 Affirmations for Money and Success 218

REFERENCES 222
Image References 222

Introduction

If you've picked up this book, then odds are you have certain dreams and hopes that are dear to you in your life. These are dreams that keep you going at the hardest of times. They are goals that you strive toward steadily and determinedly. In my experience there are two kinds of people in the world: Ones that are able to cling to their dreams, fight for their sakes, refusing to doubt their ability to achieve them and ones who see their dreams as fantasies that are nice to think about but impossible to achieve. Those who fall into the latter category often end up not being able to achieve their dreams. "I knew it was not possible," they tell themselves, not even realizing that their refusal to believe in themselves created a sort of self-fulfilling prophecy. This is the thing about dreams, you see. They are only possible to achieve when you actually believe in them and in yourself. They are only achievable when you keep an open, optimistic mind as you actively and consciously work toward them, thereby manifesting what you want to achieve.

This might sound rather far-fetched to some since it all does sound rather vague and like it's in the same realm as, say, making a wish upon a fallen star. However, the truth couldn't be farther from this because there is an abundance of scientific evidence out there proving manifestation works. Look at anything from the neurological phenomenon known as neuroplasticity to the law of attraction, which is firmly grounded in quantum physics, and you'll see that manifestation is as real as can be. What is more, it is something that anyone and everyone can make use of to craft and live the exact kind of life they want.

Not sure if you believe that? Then take a look at the life stories of some of the most successful people out there. Bill Gates, Steve Jobs, Michael

Jordan, Walt Disney, Sylvester Stallone… The one thing all these people have in common with one another is they all had dreams that they fought steadily toward. They all faced numerous, seemingly insurmountable obstacles along the way and they refused to adopt pessimistic outlooks and defeatist attitudes. Steve Jobs, for instance, dropped out of college because he did not want to financially burden his family. Walt Disney suffered a nervous breakdown and experienced bankruptcy before he became a star. Michael Jordan was actually cut from his high school basketball team and throughout the course of his career missed more than 9,000 shots (Ray, 2022). None of these things ever slowed any of these individuals down. Instead, these people and others like them grew and learned from their mistakes and failures. They used them as driving forces, rather than hindrances to keep chasing after the things they wanted. Put simply, they manifested exactly what they wanted and achieved the dreams they so ardently chased after.

As successful and awe-inspiring as these people are, they are not exceptional. Manifesting your dreams is something that each and every one of us is capable of doing. This might sound hard to believe, especially if you've grown used to the "It will never work," mindset but it is true. I should know, for I was not always the successful author that I am known as today. Having grown up in poverty and lost my parents at a very young age, my life began with a series of hurdles and setbacks. After I was diagnosed with a debilitating illness, I spent more than a year in the hospital and was made to confront my own mortality. Confronting your own mortality is something that often pushes you to re-examine and re-evaluate your life and this was as true for me as anyone else in my tender years. It was this confrontation, after all, that made me begin questioning what it was I wanted out of life and then start questing for it. It was through this search that I discovered the true power that having an optimistic mindset had to offer. The tools of an optimistic mindset, such as positive thinking and adopting constructive behaviors like Neuro-Linguistic Programming (NLP) and meditation, are the very things that not only helped me to survive the most difficult times in my life, but also to thrive through them all.

One key thing I've discovered through all of this is that an optimistic mindset can help anyone to live a truly happy and fulfilling life. This discovery has awakened a fascination with the power that our very thoughts and words wield over the lives that we lead and even the power they have to alter the lives of those around us. It is this fascination that has driven me to try to fully understand the mysterious realm known as the human mind and the way it can shape our reality through our internal vocabulary and emotions. Having come to grasp the startling and often overlooked truths behind this power, I was further driven to share that which I have learned. "No man is an island," as the old poem goes. So, how could I keep the staggering power that the optimistic mindset possesses to myself and not share it with others? This was the thought that rang clearest in my mind when I decided to sit down and write the *Optimist Mindset Bible*. This is the very point of this book.

If you've picked up the Optimist *Mindset Bible* and are currently turning its pages, then clearly the power of the optimist's mindset is something you want to explore to achieve a dream of your own. Perhaps it is your ideal career that you want to manifest in your life. Perhaps you're trying to invite the kind of love that you deserve. Perhaps it is something else entirely. Whatever it is that you're trying to achieve, you're more than capable of manifesting it in your life. All you have to do is keep turning the pages to find out how.

Chapter 1:
Mastering the Law of Attraction

All that we are is a result of what we have thought. –The Buddha

We like to believe that the way we perceive the world around us is the way that the world really is. This, however, is not exactly true. You see, everyone perceives the world around them through their own unique lens. That lens can be positive, negative, or even something in between. Our perception of the world shapes the reality that we exist in. This, in turn, affects our thoughts, how we feel about various things, and how we act and behave. Put another way, the way you see the world and the thoughts that you have, color your understanding of it and guide your actions. This right here is the very reason why the law of attraction works. The law of attraction dictates that when you think positive thoughts, you see the world in a more positive light. You feel more positive emotions, like joy and gratitude, for example. In turn, you act in ways that impact that world and you, positively and constructively. In doing so, you invite greater positivity into your life.,

This does not just work with positive thoughts and perceptions, of course. It works with negative ones as well. Just as positive thoughts encourage positive behaviors, negative ones fuel negative actions, thereby inviting more negativity into your life (Scott, 2020). Thus, negative thinking can attract all sorts of negative things that you don't want, be it illness, bad luck, or something else. Negative thinking can also cause you to adopt a more defeatist attitude, thus pushing you toward inaction, rather than action. This can keep you from going after the things that you want and make it impossible for you to draw the positive things you want, like, say a promotion, to yourself. How precisely does this law work, though? Why is it that your thoughts and mindset have the power to draw certain kinds of things to you and how can you take control of this power to manifest the things you really want? Let us find out.

What is The Law of Attraction?

The Law of Attraction essentially says that the universe creates and provides you with the very things that your thoughts revolve around. If those thoughts are positive, like about how healthy and strong you are, then the universe provides you with the health and strength you want and need. If those thoughts, however, are more negative, like how afraid you are of getting sick, then the universe creates and delivers that sickness you were fretting so much about. The central belief that the Law of Attraction is formed around is "like attracts like" (Farber, 2016). Say that you are in a crowd where you don't know anyone but end up talking with someone at the far end of the room. As you talk, you notice how like-minded you are and how many interests you share. You marvel at how the two of you were able to meet out of all these different people, but this is not all that surprising, at least not when you think about it in terms of the law of attraction. The simple explanation here is that the "like attracts like" rule came into the picture, thereby ensuring that you met.

If you're wondering how that could be possible, then we are going to have to turn briefly to quantum physics. According to physics, everything in life—from us human beings to the animals around the world and to the pebbles on the ground—is made up of energy (*Like Attracts Like*, n.d.). All living things have their own unique energy signature and vibration. Everyone's energy signature vibrates at a different setting. Think of humanity as a radio. Different frequencies, like FM and AM, get different channels. What frequency you are on, determines which channel you can get. If you want to get specific. channel—meaning if you want to attract something specific into your life—then you have to get onto the same frequency as it. To do that, you have to focus on the thing that you want. In other words, you have to think about it and think positively. That way, you sent the right frequency to the universe. That frequency will be the same or similar to the frequency at which the thing you want—let us say that it is a real good friend—vibrates. Having recognized this, that friend is inadvertently drawn to you, like at that crowded event you were attending.

How Does it Work?

According to the Law of Attraction, different things that vibrate at the same frequency are pulled toward one another. This is why positive thoughts are able to attract positive things and negative thoughts draw negative ones. What this means is simple: by thinking the right thoughts, you can manifest the right things in your life. Be that love, wealth, success, abundance, or something else.

If you want to manifest the right things, though, there are a couple of additional rules, aside from "like attracts like" you need to keep in mind. The first of these is that nature abhors a vacuum (Scott, 2020). What does that mean? In layman's terms, it means that nature and the universe dislike sudden empty spaces, as they throw things out of balance. Say that you removed something very negative from your life, like a toxic friend, for example. If left unattended, this will leave a vacuum in your life, which nature dislikes. What that vacuum will become filled with will depend entirely on what kinds of thoughts you're thinking. If you are mired in negative thoughts, then odds are that space will soon become filled by another toxic person. If you are thinking more positive thoughts, however, like how deserving you are of good friends that actually care about you, then that kind of friend is exactly what the universe will send your way. The idea that nature abhors a vacuum was born out of the fact that having an "empty" mind is simply impossible. Even when you're not consciously thinking about something, your subconscious mind is constantly working, generating thoughts, and arriving at various conclusions. Your mind may seemingly be empty but in reality, it is anything but, whether you realize it or not.

A third rule of the Law of Attraction is the present is always perfect. Contrary to what you may think, this does not mean that the present moment can never have anything wrong with it. You can be dealing with all sorts of stressful scenarios and challenges in the present moment. Still, such challenges do not negate the perfection of the moment. In other words, they cannot and should not prevent you from enjoying the moment. Finding the good side of challenging circumstances, beautiful things to appreciate, and stuff to enjoy, even when you're dealing with things is more than possible. All you need to do is figure out how to change your outlook on things, which you can do so with just a little bit of practice.

As for what that practice entails, there are a lot of things you can do to use the law of attraction. Of these, practicing positive thinking and positive self-talk are the first things that come to mind, as you'll see in the next chapter. Making mood and vision boards and thus making use of the power of visualization is another. Journaling can further help you too, as can any exercise that enables you to practice self-love and self-acceptance. It should be noted, however, that the Law of Attraction will not do much if you do not take action. Say that you won the lottery, for example, thanks to the Law of Attraction. You're holding the winning ticket in your hand. That ticket will not help you if you don't actually cash it in. Similarly, you'll not be able to win the lottery, if you don't play. The Law of Attraction only works if you think positively and then follow your positive thoughts with positive action.

What Can I Achieve with the Law of Attraction

That is all well and good but what exactly can the Law of Attraction bring you? The short answer to that question is "many different things." For instance, the Law of Attraction is known to increase your health and general well-being. This is especially true for your mental health and well-being. This is because the Law of Attraction begins with thinking positive thoughts and positive thoughts uplift your mood and improve your outlook. When that happens, more serotonin is produced in your body, which makes you feel good and keeps things like negative thoughts and stress at bay. This prevents stress from becoming a chronic issue for you. That is good news because chronic stress can lead to all sorts of mental and physical health conditions, like anxiety disorders, cardiovascular disease, high blood pressure, and more.

When you think positive thoughts, you not only protect yourself against such conditions, but you also keep yourself from doing things that could be considered self-sabotaging. People who think and believe they do not deserve good things, often end up taking actions that would keep them from getting good things, thereby creating a self-fulfilling prophecy of sorts. People who think positive thoughts, on the other hand, become able to take constructive, productive, positive actions, as you'll again see in greater detail in the next chapter. By giving themselves the ability to achieve the things they want, they increase their self-confidence and self-esteem levels, further improving their mental health in the process.

On top of ensuring your health and well-being, the Law of Attraction can allow you to manifest the wealth you want and deserve. This will not happen instantaneously. Wealth takes time and steady effort to gather and accumulate, as well as certain conscious changes to your finances. These changes can be rather small but their impact will be quite large. The Law of Attraction can allow you to clearly see what changes you need to make and then take action to make them into reality. It can help you to set financial goals for yourself and meet them over time. It can even shift your mindset to one focused on abundance, thereby keeping you on the right frequency for the thing you want.

The Law of Attraction can do a similar thing for both your career and your relationships. Where your career is concerned, it can enable you to better visualize and summon that which you want, set the goals you need to set, and work determinedly to achieve it. For this to be the case, you'll have to set both long and short-term goals that are specific, realistic, and achievable, which will become clearer to you in later chapters. As for relationships, the Law of Attraction can aid you as you set personal goals for this too. In addition to that, it can draw your attention to the various fears and hesitations that might be holding you back, like a fear of intimacy, for example, or a fear of getting hurt. This, in turn, can help you to consciously work on them. This will make it possible for you to see what healthy relationships are supposed to look and feel like. Having experienced this, you'll be able to cultivate it for yourself and then focus on strengthening the bonds you've forged. Thus, the Law of Attraction will make the relationships you wish you could have into a reality that already exists in your life.

How precisely can you use the Law of Attraction to manifest these different things? To answer this question, we will have to take a closer look at the art of manifestation and how it works in relation to the things that you want, starting with that seemingly elusive concept: Love.

Chapter 2:
Manifesting Love

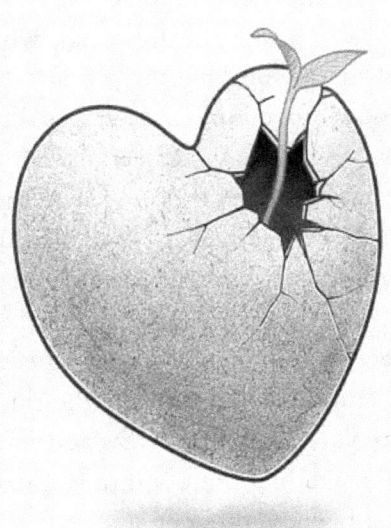

Your task is not to seek love, but merely to seek and find all the barriers within yourself that you've built against it. –Rumi

Love is at once one of the simplest and most complex, even mystifying things out in the world. It is a feeling that has inspired who knows how many songs and poems, giving birth to how many countless works of art. Love is something we are all, even the most skeptical among us, searching for, whether we are ready to acknowledge it or not. This is because while love is very hard to define and explain, at least on a rational level, it is a natural part of our being. On a biological level, we all crave love, because we have an inherent need for both affection and relationships. If we want to understand what love really is and how we can manifest it in our lives, we must first grasp where our need for it even comes from.

Every human being on planet Earth craves affection, which is an absolute requirement of any healthy relationship, whatever form that relationship may take. Strictly speaking, affection is not an emotion. Rather, it is a feeling of connection, of having a bond which exists between two people (Rhodes, 2017). Affection can exist on various levels. After all, the affection you feel for one friend may be different to what you feel for another. In the same way, your affection level for your parents and siblings is bound to be very different from what you feel for your friends and your spouse. Affection, then, is relationship-specific, at least in its level of intimacy. Simultaneously, it is something you give, just as much as you take. If emotions like love are the things that you feel, then affection is the work you put in to express and show that feeling. It is how you tell the person standing right before you that you care about them, as well as their well-being and happiness.

Human beings need affection because it makes them feel safe, secure, and wanted. When you show affection to others, you give the people around you the message that the two of you are compatible. This creates a sense of peace and harmony in your relationship, allowing it to grow stronger over time. Furthermore, affection helps you to determine and draw your emotional boundaries with different people and understand how far we are willing to go for different individuals. Put simply, affection and by extension, love are things that you need to form strong, healthy relationships and look after your emotional well-being.

The thing is a lot of people forget that "manifesting" love requires giving affection, as much as receiving it. A great deal more people overlook the fact that in order to manifest love in their lives, they must first learn how to show and give it to themselves. As Stephen Chbosky said, this is because "We accept the love we think we deserve" (Chbosky, 1999). So, how could you manifest the healthy, affectionate love you want in your life if you do not recognize that you deserve it and start by showing it to yourself? Manifesting love in your life begins with practicing self-love and accepting that you are deserving of it. It can further be manifested by showing the people you love that you truly care about them. How could you go about doing these things then? What steps do you really need to take to invite more and greater love into your life?

How Can You Manifest Love?

The first step to manifesting love is to start practicing self-love. Unfortunately, self-love is something many of us struggle with. You might find it hard to feel worthy of love if you've recently had your heart and trust broken by someone. You might similarly find it difficult if you are the type of person to put other people's needs and wants above your own, as though they are always more important. The primary reason why most of us struggle with self-love though is simple: It is because we have convinced ourselves that practicing self-love is a selfish thing to do. This couldn't be farther from the truth because being able to love and care for yourself is something that opens you up to loving and caring for others. Not only that, but self-love is a practice that increases your capability of inviting love into your life.

Self-love is something that allows you to take care of yourself on a physical, emotional, and mental level. Studies show that self-love helps keep our stress levels down, which is important because stress can wreak havoc on your immune system and your mental health. It reduces the amount of harmful behavior you engage in and promotes helpful behavior. Harmful behavior includes self-sabotaging acts like smoking and drinking, mind you, which means that self-love is doubly good for your health. Meanwhile, this practice and belief helps you to develop self-compassion and, most importantly, resilience. Resilience is important because it is the thing that keeps us going at the toughest and most stressful of times (Waters, 2020). It is what makes it possible for you to still enjoy the moment that you are living in, despite the anxieties that might be part of your life for the time being.

One of the most important benefits of self-love, though, is that it makes it possible for you to manifest the kind of love you want in your life. Self-love can, in many ways, be considered the key to manifestation, regardless of what you're manifesting. The reason for this is simple: Self-love is all about believing and accepting what you truly deserve. To manifest something you have to get onto the same wavelength as it, as you know. To manifest healthy love in its various forms—relationships and friendships, for example—you have to start sending out the right energy signals for it. Think about it this way: If the thoughts circulating through your head are all about how lazy or clumsy or "insert negative adjective here" you are, then will that vibrational signature attract the people who will show you care, kindness, and attention to your life? Unfortunately, it will not. Instead, it will attract people that validate those negative thoughts and beliefs you're having about yourself. These people's behavior will then make you feel even worse about yourself and pretty soon you'll be stuck in a devastating feedback loop that kind of resembles a whirlpool in that it sucks you deeper and deeper in.

Practicing Self-Love

Practicing self-love, then, helps you get on the right vibrational frequency to attract the love you need. So, how can you practice self-love if you've trouble with it in the first place? One of the chief things you can do to practice self-love more is to make a point of prioritizing your mental and physical health and well-being. The undeniable fact of the matter is that your mental and physical health are directly and intricately connected to how you feel on a day-to-day basis on a physical, mental and emotional level. Doing something as simple yet necessary as keeping a healthy diet and a regular sleep schedule can work wonders in all these regards. The same can be said for exercising regularly, which is known to decrease the stress hormone known as cortisol. This helps you to manage stress, as well as other mental health disorders, like anxiety, for example. So does going to therapy, if you are able to do it.

The reason why all of these actions are considered self-love practices is that they give you the message "I am important and deserve to be taken good care of." They follow up and reinforce this message through the power of actions, making you believe it even more as time goes by. This predictably increases the value you place in yourself and thus, how much you love yourself. By the rule of the law of attraction, this enables you to draw people to your life that will value and love you in the same way. Practicing self-compassion as an extension of self-love will achieve the same result. Self-compassion is your ability to acknowledge when you make a mistake or fail at something without berating yourself.

Imagine that you are talking to a friend and they tell you about a mistake they made. How would you respond to them? Would you point out that they tried their best and approach them with kindness or would you agree that they messed up and are horrible for messing up? Odds are, you'd do the latter because you care about your friend. The thing is, though, most of us do not show such kindness for ourselves when we make a mistake. Instead, we engage in heavy self-criticism, get angry at ourselves, and even condemn ourselves. As a result, we lose some of our self-confidence and experience all sorts of negative emotions. If we want to practice self-love and thus begin manifesting love in our lives, we must decidedly refrain from doing this. Put another way, we must practice self-compassion and treat ourselves the same way we would treat a valued friend. This might be a little difficult to do at first, especially if you've grown used to heavy self-criticism. However, the more you keep at it, the better you'll get at practicing self-compassion. The more you practice self-compassion, the more you'll practice self-love as well.

Another thing you can do to show yourself more self-love is to stop comparing yourself to others. Again, this might be rather difficult to do since it has likely become a habit, especially since the existence of things like social media make it so easy to do. However, it is very necessary if you want to manifest the kind of love that you deserve. The thing about comparing yourself to others is that it can cause you a great deal of stress (Scott, 2020b). Over time, that stress can chip away at your sense of self-esteem. Thoughts such as "Why can't I be that smart/successful/insert-adjective-here" will keep popping into your mind, whittling down your self-confidence too. This can cause you to engage in more and more negative thoughts about yourself until your reserves of self-love and confidence begin to deplete.

A final self-love practice that can help you to manifest love in your life is to learn to draw boundaries. Contrary to what you might think, boundaries are very healthy for you. Having boundaries with people does not mean you do not love or care about them. It simply means you value your own needs and are willing to prioritize them and thus yourself. Thanks to this, setting boundaries allows you to get into healthy relationships where you, your needs, and your limitations are respected. The thing to remember about boundaries is that they change from person to person. The boundaries you set for a good friend are going to be the same as the ones you set for a colleague you do not know very well. Likewise, they will be different from the boundaries you have with your partner. That is perfectly normal and understandable since the nature of your relationship with these people will be inherently different.

That you'll have different boundaries with different people means that you might agree to do something for, say, your brother but not for the friend of a friend. However, regardless of how close you are with someone you'll inevitably say "no" to some of their requests. You'll do this because that way you'll be able to make sure you only do things that you are truly comfortable with and that is what boundaries are all about. You cannot have a relationship, at least not a healthy one, where you place someone's needs and wants above your own all of the time. If you did, then the message you gave yourself would be, "My needs and wants are not important." A natural extension of this line of thinking is "I am not important", which is not exactly conducive for practicing self-love or manifesting love for that matter.

How do you go about doing all this though? Saying that you should prioritize self-love is easy, after all. Saying that you should stop comparing or that you should practice self-compassion is even easier. Putting these things into practice is where things get difficult. The good news is that there are certain techniques, which you can use regularly and make part of your everyday schedule, that can help you with all of this, starting with shadow work and positive self-talk.

Getting Clarity and Shadow Work

First things first, if you want to start manifesting love in your life, you first need to gain more clarity on what it is you want and need. What does "love" mean to you? What needs do you need to have met in a loving, caring relationship? More importantly, why do you need these things? Manifesting love—or anything else for that matter—requires knowing exactly what you want, be it a new partner, someone who speaks the same love language as you, a healthier relationship than the ones in your past, or something else entirely. That is the only way you can start sending out the exact energy you need to draw that thing to you. The more vaguely you express your needs and desires, the harder it will be to draw them to you. The more concrete, visible, and defined they are, the more pronounced their energy signature will be and the more quickly they will come your way.

Put simply, then, you have to manifest love with conscious intention. To do this you have to ask yourself what you want and why you want them. Then, you have to strive to answer those questions. One thing that can help you a great deal in this process is to write down the answers to your questions and edit them until they are as specific as they can be.

Let us say that one of the answers you end up writing down is "I want a partner who is more considerate of my emotional needs." It is great that you've determined this but how do you attract such a thing into your life? You start by taking care of your emotional needs more. You take this a step further by doing some self-reflection and considering how you behave toward others. Are you more selfish or giving? More generous or stingy? Approachable or closed off? Remember, the traits that you display are bound to attract people displaying the same traits. So, if you are more selfish and closed off in your behavior, you'll end up drawing similar kinds of people to your life. How likely will it be for such people to be considerate of your emotional needs? The answer to that question is "not very."

Once you've gained clarity of what you want, you need to gain a greater understanding of what kind of person you are. To that end, you can reflect on who you think you are. What are your defining traits? You can also consider whether you're in an emotionally, physically, and mentally healthy place right now or not. If not, then these are things you want to work on so that you can practice self-love and start manifesting. This kind of work can be difficult, of course, because it entails looking at and seeing your more negative sides. Confronting these negative aspects of ourselves can be really hard. A lot of us have the tendency to deny or ignore parts of ourselves that we do not really like, you see. We like to pretend that we are less stingy than we are or that we do not habitually self-sabotage. We do such things because we do not want to meet other people's or even our own disapproval. We also do so in an effort to avoid possible rejection.

Car Jung, the psychologist, defines these characteristics and traits that you repress or ignore as your shadow self. Your shadow self is like a bundle of your greatest insecurities and worries (Perry, 2015). It is something you keep in the dark to protect yourself from the pain it can cause you. Unfortunately, this does not mean they go away. Instead, they fester where they lie, affecting your emotional well-being and even the way you behave toward others, which in turn affects the kind of relationships you are in. If you want to prevent this from being the case, then what you need to do is become more aware of your shadow self and treat it with compassion. This does not mean you shouldn't work on your more negative traits, of course. You absolutely should if you want to manifest love. It just means that you should be compassionate and accepting toward yourself in the meantime.

This is where shadow work comes in, which can help you to plainly see the parts of yourself that you might not like too much but be accepting and compassionate toward yourself nonetheless. It can do so by reframing your shadow traits as things to work on and improve, rather than as weaknesses or signs that you're a "bad" person. To practice shadow work, you need to, as always, ask yourself some questions, starting with "What do I consider to be my negative traits?" (Gilbert, 2022). These can be either traits that you hide or ones that other people tell you're "bad". Another way of identifying shadow traits might be to ask yourself what are some of the things that other people do that annoy or discomfit you? The things that annoy you are all too often the very things that you have a tendency toward and that you try to cover up. If it annoys you when people are unambitious or lazy, for example, then those are likely shadow traits you possess as well.

Once you've identified different traits, you can get to work on getting down to their roots, because that is the only way to resolve them. One question you might ask yourself in this situation is who taught you to repress a certain treat, either consciously or unconsciously. You can also ask yourself whether you hide this trait consciously or subconsciously and what kinds of feelings and sensations it raises within you. For instance, if the trait in question is laziness, then perhaps it evokes feelings of unworthiness or failure within you.

Having identified the complex array of feelings your shadow traits spark, you can at last move onto resolving them. You can do this by trying several different tactics. A most basic one is to ask yourself if there are any good sides to the trait in question. If you're considering "laziness", then perhaps one good side to it might be that it can keep you from overworking yourself and thus, burning out? Finding the good side of a shadow trait might be a little difficult, but it will not be impossible to do. It will just require some careful thought and consideration.

Another question you should ask yourself about your shadow traits is how you might turn them into sources of strength. That might sound a little oxymoron-ish, but—again—take laziness as an example. Could you use this trait to determine when you should slow things down a bit and take a breath? Could it be part of your everyday strategy, ensuring you take regular breaks as you work, which are proven to increase your motivation and productivity, anyways?

A final interesting question you might ask yourself about your shadow traits is how you might actively turn these traits into sources of strength. How can you cultivate and use their positive sides? Having determined these things, you can start putting them into practice whenever you feel the urge to repress one characteristic or other. In doing so, you can slowly increase your level of self-love and start manifesting more love in your life. If you find that you still struggle with this, that is alright to be expected, really. You can't go from repressing yourself in various ways to immediately accepting yourself as you're at the drop of a hat. You can get better and better at doing so, though, with the help of positive self-talk.

Manifesting Love With Positive Self-Talk

Self-talk can be defined as the way in which you talk to yourself. We all have an inner monologue that runs through our heads practically all day long, at least when we are awake. This monologue is referred to as self-talk. Self-talk can be split into two categories: positive and negative. Positive self-talk is an inner monologue that supports you and is self-affirming (York Morris, 2016). Negative self-talk, known alternatively as rumination, is the kind of inner monologue that puts you down. If you're replaying an embarrassing thing that happened the other day over and over again in your mind, then that is an example of negative self-talk. So are thinking thoughts like "I can't believe I did that. I am so stupid," or "I am never going to be able to get this right."

As a general rule, you want to use positive self-talk, rather than negative self-talk. This is because positive self-talk is known to increase your happiness, well-being, and self-love levels, making it easier for you to manifest love. One study, for example, has found that self-love actually reduces stress and keeps it from becoming chronic (Scott, 2019). This is because positive self-talk enables you to perceive others and the events unfolding around you in a more positive light, whereas negative self-talk does not. When you keep thinking negative thoughts, you attribute more negative intentions to the people around you, even when they are well-meaning. Hence, you become far less likely to believe in and accept the genuine love they have to offer you, which is hardly conducive for manifesting love.

At the same time, you become less able to handle the challenges that come your way in life and become more accustomed to seeing the negatives, rather than the positives of a situation. If you are in a relationship and are prone to negative self-talk, for example, you'll be more likely to replay something negative that happened between you and your partner over and over again in your head, then to remember the good things that happened with them that day. Getting more affected by and hung up on those negative incidents, you'll be likely to convince yourself that that relationship is going nowhere and thus to either sabotage it or end it.

Positive self-talk can prevent all this from happening. On top of that, it can boost your self-confidence and self-esteem levels (Mead, 2019). This is important because people who have high levels of self-confidence and self-esteem are more likely to meet the goals that they set for themselves. Most importantly, though, such people inevitably end up building stronger and more loving relationships with others and themselves. After all, who does not want to be around someone who's positive overall, confident, self-assured, and happy with who they are? A study from 2013 is evidence enough of this, since it found that couples who are prone to think positively are more likely to cooperate with one another to solve whatever issues that they encounter. As a result, such couples are far more likely to resolve their issues and stay together for a long time to come.

It can be said, then, that positive self-talk can help you to manifest love in one of two ways: It can make it easier to see, embrace, and use the positive sides of your so-called "negative" traits and it can help you draw a positive, healthy kind of love into your life by altering the way in which you think and see the world. For this to happen, though, you need to first figure out how you're going to turn negative self-talk into positive self-talk. There are a number of good techniques you can use to do this. The first is to become aware of those moments when you're thinking negatively and identify what kind of negative thought you are having. Negative self-talk falls into one of four categories, these being

- catastrophizing
- polarizing
- magnifying
- personalizing

Catastrophizing means immediately jumping to the worst case scenario when something happens. If you and your partner were to have a fight over something trivial, for example, and you now keep thinking, "They are going to break up with me, it is over," then that is an example of catastrophizing. Polarizing means seeing things only in black and white with no gray areas in between. It is the kind of thought you often engage with when you make a mistake and start thinking of yourself as a failure. A polarizing mind does not consider a mistake as something that happens to everyone nor as a learning opportunity to use and grow from. Rather, it sees it as something a bit unforgivable. Magnifying, meanwhile, equals blowing things out of proportion and focusing only on the negatives of a situation and not at all on the positives. As for personalizing, that means blaming yourself for every little thing that goes wrong, even when it is not remotely your fault. You can imagine how exhausting that can get.

If you are prone to negative self-talk, then it is vital that you get to work identifying the kind of negative thoughts you've been having. This is important because a lot of the time, we do not notice that the thoughts that we are having are negative. Neither do we notice just how often we think negative thoughts throughout the day. Once you do start noticing, though, it becomes impossible to ignore. A great way to start taking more notice is to carry a little notebook with you and write down a negative thought every time you have it. This will make turning said thought into a more positive one, which you'll learn how to do momentarily, into an easier process. As you write down your negative thoughts, consider what kind of negative self-talk it counts as. Then place that label directly next to it. This will enable you to figure out where that thought is coming from, what kinds of situations trigger such thoughts, and how you can reframe them.

Situations that trigger negative self-talk are referred to as "self-talk traps" in psychology. Certain situations trigger negative self-talk more often than others. What those situations are changes from person to person. Someone with social anxiety, for instance, might fall into a self-talk trap when they have to attend a crowded networking event. Someone else who finds it hard to be vulnerable might have more negative thoughts when they start a new relationship. The trick to avoid falling into a self-talk trap is to find what yours are. To accomplish this, all you have to do is take a look at those negative thoughts you've been recording. What are they about, for the most part. Are there any specific events, occurrences, or situations that have triggered them? If so, what kind of situations were they? After you answer these questions, you'll be able to determine exactly what kinds of circumstances trigger your negative thoughts. Knowing what is coming, you'll thus become more ready to actively put a stop to them.

What if you are unsure if a thought you're having is positive or negative, though? Such things can happen, since negative self-talk does not always involve blatant self-criticism, though it can. One thing you can do when you're struggling to determine the nature of a thought is to question it. How does this thought make you feel? Are those feelings more positive or negative? If a friend were to say the thought that you're having out loud, what would you say to them? Would you discourage them from saying such things? If so, then that is a big sign you are engaging in negative self-talk.

As for how to stop negative self-talk, there are two strategies you can adopt to do this. The first is to question the validity of that though. A query as simple as "Is this thought real?" can be more effective than you'd think. Let us say that one thought you'd like to put an end to is "I am not a lovable person." What evidence do you have that actually supports this? What evidence do you have that runs counter to it? By asking yourself these two questions and then honestly answering them, you'll come to see that you actually do not have much, if any evidence, that proves your thought. You have plenty of evidence that disproves it though, which means that this negative thought is not real. The thing about negative, absolute thoughts like this, though, is that they can feel pretty real. This feeling can be dissipated through cold, hard facts and evidence. If you want to take things a step further, you can always start writing down your two evidence lists. This way, you'll have concrete, hard to ignore proofs that dismantle your negative thoughts. You can turn these proofs whenever the same kinds of negative thoughts arise in your mind, until you can quiet down your mind at last.

The second strategy you can adopt to change negative self-talk into positive self-talk is to physically alter them. Remember how you wrote down your negative thoughts in a little notebook? Well, this exercise entails writing down their more positive or at the very least neutral versions directly opposite them. The idea here is to notice every time you've a negative thought, then consciously change it into a positive one. This might be slow going and a bit hard at first, but the more you do it, the easier it will get. Pretty soon, the number of negative thoughts you jot down in your notebook will decrease. After a certain point, you'll find that you're thinking less and less negatively and that your mindset has become far more positive and even optimistic. Your conscious efforts to change your negative way of thinking will have sunk into your subconscious mind, making positive thoughts a more deeply ingrained part of it.

As for how exactly you might replace negative thoughts with positive ones, let us take a look at some examples:

Negative Self-Talk	Positive Self-Talk
I am such an idiot.	I did not do as well as I could have but that is perfectly alright. Now, I know what I need to do differently next time.
I am inherently unlovable.	I am worthy and deserving of being loved and capable of loving in turn.
I really messed things up.	I made a mistake but it is something I can learn and grow from.
I'll never be able to get this done on time.	I have a lot to do but I can get through as much of it as I can. It will all work out so long as I keep my co-workers updated on my progress.
What is the point, no one wants to talk to me anyways.	There will be at least one person that I can meet that would like to get to know me and that I'll click with. All I have to do is put myself out there a little.
I can't do this.	I can do this; all I have to do is try.
I am never going to get any better at this.	I will get better and better at this, so long as I keep trying.
I knew I couldn't do it.	It is alright if I couldn't get this perfectly on the first try, as I will grow and learn from it.

Now that you know what negative self-talk can look like once it has been transformed into positive self-talk, it is time to try your hand at it. Let us see how you might transform the following negative thoughts:

- I can't do anything right. I shouldn't even try:

  _____

  _____

- I do not like anything at all about myself:

  _____

  _____

- I am so incompetent:

  _____

  _____

- I am such a failure:

  _____

  _____

The thing to remember about positive self-talk is that it will not really stick and become your go-to method of thinking without constant repetition. It is that which is repeated over and over in your mind that becomes ingrained in it. That is likely how you got into the habit of thinking negative thoughts and manifesting the "wrong" kind of love in the first place. It is how you'll manifest the right kind of love—the kind you deserve and want—too. Now, it might be that you're hesitant to believe all this. After all, could the words and phrases you repeat to yourself really help you manifest whatever you want? Truthfully, there are many stories illustrating just how well self-talk can work in this regard. The most impressive example out of all of them, however, must be a story that Marilyn Monroe shared with a journalist several years ago.

As the story goes, one day Monroe and a friend of hers were walking down the street. At the time, Monroe was one of the most famous actresses in the country, if not the most famous one. Despite this and despite the fact that Monroe was not wearing any kind of disguise like a hat and sunglasses, for example, no one even looked their way. When her friend remarked on the matter, Monroe asked her if she would like for her to "Turn Marilyn on"? When her friend said that she did, Marilyn paused for a moment and started whispering to herself. When her friend paid attention she realized that Marilyn was repeating things like how she was a goddess, the absolute epitome on feminine beauty to herself over and over again. After a little while, Marilyn stopped and kept walking down the street. This time when she did, all heads suddenly turned her way. Everyone suddenly started noticing her and people flocked to their side to get her autograph and express their admiration. Things became so hectic that Marilyn and her friend were not able to take a single step without someone rushing over to their side. This, right, here, is the power of positive self-talk and repetition. It is also why positive self-talk is known by another name in certain circles: The Marilyn Effect (Lamont, 2022).

As useful as it is, positive self-talk is not the only tool you can use to manifest love. As a general rule, the more you are able to believe in that which you want, the more quickly you'll be able to draw it to you. So, what is the most believable thing in your life? That which you can see, of course, since seeing is believing and all that.

The Power of Visualization

As human beings, we all have certain mental tools and techniques at our disposal that we can use to craft the exact kind of life we want to lead. Positive self-talk is obviously one of these tools, but so is visualization. This tool, which pairs exceptionally well with positive self-talk, has long since proven that it can help you manifest an array of different things, including love. Before we get to how it can do so, though, let us first understand what, precisely it is. Visualization is a mental technique where you picture the exact thing you want to have in your life (Moe, 2021). You create a mental picture of that thing and bring it to your mind on a regular, at least daily basis.

Visualization can be divided into two categories. These categories are outcome visualization and process visualization. As you might have guessed from those names, outcome visualization entails imagining the end result of something. So, if you were running a race and imagining yourself winning first place, then that would be an example of outcome visualization. Process visualization, on the other hand, entails picturing how a certain event or process will unfold. If you were imagining running that race you were going to participate in and imagine how things would go during the race, then that would be an example of process visualization.

Whatever kind of visualization you use—for best results you should use both, mind you, but more on that later—there is no question that this technique works. This is because visualization is a great way of getting your mind to focus on the things that matter most to you. That matters because here is the thing about the human brain: it can't actually tell the difference between what is real and what is imaginary. Your conscious brain can, do not get me wrong, but your subconscious mind can't. So, when you imagine a specific scenario unfolding, like winning a race, your subconscious mind takes it to be real. As a result, the neurons in your brain that are associated with the actions you need to take for that scenario to actually happen begin firing like mad. Thus, your brain starts doing the mental work required to win that race and prepares your body to actually do it when the time comes. By the time that race rolls around, your mind and body are both ready to run it. After all, they have done so countless times by now and won countless times to boot.

Visualization, then, can be very effective in getting you ready to achieve the future you want and obtain the things you want to obtain. Just ask LeBron James and Michael Pheps, who are both professional athletes that regularly use the power of visualization to achieve the victories they want. Visualization does not just help you to manifest the thing you want, though. It does all sorts of additional things like boost your self-confidence and reduce stress and anxiety, thereby increasing your levels of self-love as well.

The thing about visualization is that it has to be as specific as it possibly can be for it to be effective. The more specific your vision, you see, the more real it will feel to you and your brain. Given that, you shouldn't just picture how the thing you're trying to obtain and achieve will look like. Instead, you should use all your senses in your visualization practice. Say that you are visualizing the perfect first date. Don't just picture how things will look at the restaurant you go to. Try to hear the sounds around you, like people eating, the conversation between you and your partner, and how their laughter will sound when you tell a joke. Try to imagine the different scents around you, like their perfume or cologne, the aroma wafting from the food you'll be eating, and perhaps the crisp night air as you walk back from the restaurant. Likewise, focus on touch and taste, trying to feel how warm their hand will be in yours and how the food or perhaps later your first kiss will taste like. Try to pack as many sensory details into what you're visualizing as possible so as to make it as real and believable as possible. That way, you'll be able to truly leverage the power this technique has to offer you.

Another way to make something you're visualizing more realistic is to imagine the emotion you'd feel when experiencing it. If you are visualizing a race, the emotions attached to it may be triumph, victory, and joy. If you are visualizing a good first date, it may be excitement and butterflies in your stomach. Whatever the event, imagining and trying to feel the emotions that come with it can make your visualization practice more realistic. At the same time, it can draw events and incidents that would evoke those very emotions to your life, helping you to manifest them.

Visualization is most effective if it is done with some regularity. Ideally, you want to visualize for around 10 minutes in one go. You also want to engage in this practice about twice a day, though you can do so more often if you'd like. Starting your day with a morning visualization practice in bed, coupled with some breathing exercise can be a very good way of setting the mood for the day. Likewise, ending your day with some visualization practices is a good idea, as it can bring things to a calm, pleasant close. If you're unsure of what precisely you want to visualize, one great exercise to try out is something called the Pink Balloon. The Pink Balloon is especially good for night-time, as in right before you drift off to sleep. This is a simple but very powerful exercise that is known to both help manifest love and make it easier for you to fall asleep (Hurst, 2016).

To start, lie down in your bed in a comfortable position and take a couple of deep, relaxing breaths. As you breathe in and out, picture a pink balloon in your mind's eye. This pink balloon represents love, hence its color. Now, as you breathe in and out, picture the balloon slowly inflating, filling not with air but with your intentions to manifest love. Picture it growing bigger and bigger. Once it is sufficiently big enough, imagine yourself letting go of the string it is attached to. See the balloon drift up toward the sky, slowly climbing higher and higher as the minutes trickle by. The balloon drifting farther away is a good thing because that means it is going out into the universe to find the person that is exactly right for you and is truly deserving of your love.

The Pink Balloon is not the only visualization exercise that you could try. There are many others and a curious number of them involve writing. This makes sense when you think about it. After all, putting something in writing often makes it that much more real. What is more, writing a scene or moment that you are visualizing allows you to get more descriptive and detailed with it and thus see it better in your mind's eye. So, what should you write about when you are visualizing love? Sure, you can write about what your partner should look like but leaving it at that would be a little ephemeral and rather limiting. You might miss out on actual possibilities if you focus too much on such things. What you really want to focus on when visualizing love is how you want your partner to make you feel. For example, you probably want to feel safe—both emotionally and physically—with your partner. You want to feel that you can be the person that you really are when you're with them. These kinds of feelings are exactly what you should visualize and write about.

One way you could do this is to write down all the things you want in your future partner, starting with how you want to feel with them. As a rule, you should keep this list general, rather than envision someone with a specific hair color or of a specific height. You can also write about what qualities are most important in a person for you. How important is reliability to you, for example? How about decisiveness? Is it really important for you to be with someone who can make you laugh or who you can goof off with sometimes? Is it vital that they be emotionally open and able to be vulnerable? Making a list answering such questions will both help you to better visualize what you want and gain greater clarity on it. To take this a step further, you can create a similar list describing your ideal relationship (Salmansohn, 2015).

The more you engage in writing oriented visualization practices like this, the more you'll be able to manifest love. Not only that, but you'll find that you become a happier person overall. This is because the loving future you envision for yourself will dismantle and whittle away at your fears, anxieties, and any emotional pain—like the kind you're likely to go through following a break-up—you may be experiencing. The optimistic attitude that visualization practices support even have an impact on your brain health, as studies show. There is one study, for instance, that proves imagining positive things on a regular basis—meaning practicing visualization regularly—increases the blood flow to parts of your brain that control more positive emotions and functions. At the same time, it decreases the blood flow to regions of the brain in charge of more negative ones (Morita et al., 2016).

Having sung praises for visualization techniques involving writing, it must be said that not everyone is a fan of the act. Some people would rather not pick up a pen and paper or open up a Word Doc on their computer and that is perfectly fine. Luckily, there are plenty of other love visualization exercises you can try if you fall into this category of people. Take the "Open Your Heart by Opening Doors" practice. This practice involves picturing yourself standing in front of a door. Take your time visualizing the door and what it looks and even feels like. Remember, the more realistic a visualization exercise, the better it will be. Try to be as detailed as you possibly can be since it will represent the excitement and hope you hold for the future. Finally, picture yourself opening the door. Start by imagining the feel of the handle in your hand—how is it shaped, is it cool to the touch?—the creak of the door as it opens, whether you have to pull or push the door to open it, how heavy it is… Finally, visualize what you'll see waiting for you on the other side (Hurst, 2016).

Another exercise you can try is to work on removing any limiting beliefs you may have that are preventing you from manifesting love. Limiting beliefs are the negative thoughts that you've, like "I am not deserving of love," that keep you from manifesting the things you want. One way to dismantle beliefs like this is through positive self-talk, as you now know. Another is to examine them more closely in writing. To that end, you can question where these thoughts have come from. When exactly did you start thinking about these things? What are your reasons for rejecting them? That done, you can make a conscious commitment to look for reasons to reject them every single day. Some days may be harder than others, but truthfully, it will get easier because such a commitment will force you to take notice of reasons you otherwise might have overlooked. Again, engaging in this practice in writing can make it even more effective (Hurst, 2016b).

Just as there are writing-focused visualization exercises, there are also image-focused ones. These are practices like vision boards that involve creating something that you can look at and physically see every day, rather than just dreaming up something in your imagination. Vision boards work because they are visual reminders of the things you are seeking to achieve and the intentions that you hold. A love vision board can help you in a number of different ways. It can give you greater clarity on what you want in a relationship, for one (Feyoh, 2022). It can make you discover and see things about yourself that you had not realized before, like values that are important to you and what your relationship priorities are. Most importantly, it can become a symbolic representation of the kind of love you want, putting the energy you need to attract it out into the universe.

There is no "right" way to create a vision board. There is only your way. You can create a physical vision board on cardboard or some other similar material just as you can create one on your computer, using Pinterest. You can use any kind of design and style you want too. A good start might be to place the word "Love" at the center of your board, written in a font that you like. Then you can start building around it using images, photos, illustrations, quotes, and whatever else you'd like. These visuals should remind you of what love means to you. Alternatively, they can be representations of your ideal partner or ideal relationship.

Let us say you're creating a vision board to manifest the kind of partner you want to have. How do you choose the right images? First, you write down all the qualities that you want your future partner to have. Again, this does not mean listing things like "blue eyes" and "six feet tall". Rather, it means listing those vital qualities you want in a partner, like trustworthiness, compassion, vulnerability, and honesty. You can similarly list the values you want your future partner to have, along with where you'd like your partner to be in five, ten, or even twenty years from now (Cyrene, 2019). Now comes the slightly tricky part: What images, words, and quotes represent all these different things. To find the right visuals, you'll have to go on a bit of a hunt on Google or through various magazines, if you want to be a little old school about it. Then you have to choose the ones that feel right to you. For instance, if you want a partner that is family oriented, one image that might symbolize that might be that of a father playing with their children. Once you have gotten all the images you wanted, the only thing left to do will be to start arranging them on your vision board. This is a purely aesthetic thing, which means you can go about it however you'd like.

A vision board does not just have to be for single people though. Someone in a relationship can create one as well. The thing about manifesting love is that it does not just end when you get the kind of relationships and friendships you want to be in. Love is something that you have to continually manifest, just as relationships are things you always have to work on. Hence, there is nothing strange about a couple creating a vision board, nor is there anything off about them writing a love mission statement. A love mission statement is a very important visualization and manifestation tool because it helps people in a relationship define the destination they want to head to and make sure their goals and expectations are all aligned (Gamades, 2021). This is why couples therapists often have the couples they work with create such statements.

Step #1 for writing your own love mission statement is, as before, to define your and your partner's core values. Your core values are the things that are the most important to you. What you want to do here is to capture a value in a single word—like "honesty" or "generosity", for example—and come up with a total of 15 to 20 of them. Having done that, you can move onto step #2, which is to narrow down that list to five or six values that are important to you as a couple. Finding similarities here works but you might also spot a value on your partner's personal list and realize how important it is to you too.

After that comes step #3: Defining your purpose as a couple. Identifying your purpose can be tough, but there are some questions you can ask yourself to make things easier. Some examples of such questions might be:

- What do we consider our couples' purpose to be?
- What are the things we are both passionate about?
- What are the things that we really believe in?
- How do we want to be remembered?

So, you have identified your core couples' values and now roughly know what your purpose is. This brings you to step #4, which is to actually write your mission statement, using what you've learned. A mission statement typically covers three things: what you want to accomplish, who you're doing all this for, and how will the things you are doing make your and your partner's lives better. The goal here is to capture the answer to these three questions in two to three sentences at most. You can feel free to create multiple drafts of your work, of course. Once you arrive at a result that you really find satisfactory, though, then you'll have gotten your perfect mission statement. You'll then be able to use it as a kind of guide or compass in your relationship. That compass will point the way toward the way you want your relationship to really be, both putting out the right energy out there for it to come true and nudging you toward taking the actions you need to if you want to have that relationship.

Believing and Embodying

Yet another manifestation technique you can use to invite love into your life is using affirmations. Affirmations, or positive affirmation as they are otherwise known, are simple phrases that you say to yourself. You can repeat affirmations either inside your mind or out loud. You can even write them down and plaster them where you'll easily be able to see them every day. Like positive self-talk, affirmations challenge the various negative thoughts you have on a daily basis (Moore, 2019). If you are skeptical about how well they work, then all you have to do is take a look at the copious amount of research that was done about them. One study, for example, found that when you practice affirmations, a part of your brain called the ventromedial prefrontal cortex suddenly becomes very active.

This mouthful of a region in your brain controls your ability to process information that is related to yourself. In other words, when this region becomes more active, you become more able to value yourself. This impacts your mental health and well-being in several ways. It decreases your stress levels, for starters, which makes sense since it would be hard to feel stressed when you're feeling really good about yourself. It makes it easier for you to accept mistakes and even failure by making you see them as growth opportunities. At the same time, it increases your resilience in the face of tough situations, such as a break up, making things easier to bear. Most importantly, though, positive affirmations put you into a more optimistic mindset, allowing you to manifest whatever your heart desires.

So, how, precisely, do positive affirmations help you to manifest love? The key to using affirmations to manifest love lies in understanding one of the most basic rules of manifestation: Like attracts like. If you repeat to yourself that you are loveable and cherished, then you're going to attract people that will love and cherish you into your life. If you're constantly thinking about how unlovable you're, then you're going to attract people who just will not value you in your life. Their treatment of you'll thus turn into a kind of self-fulfilling prophecy, proving to you just how "unlovable" you are. See the problematic trap here?

Attracting the kind of love you want requires altering your mindset and that is where affirmations come in. One other region of your brain that affirmations are known to affect your brain's pleasure center. This means that affirmations have the power to make you feel really good each time you repeat them to yourself (Hampton, 2019). Affirmations, then, help you to attract two different things at once: They help you attract whatever it is you want—in this case, love—and they help you attract things that make you feel good by making you feel good. In other words, they get two birds with one stone.

As with positive self-talk and visualization, though, you need to use affirmations every single day for this to actually be the case. Repeating your affirmations in the morning, when you've just woken up or when you are getting ready for the day is a great idea since it will put you in the right, optimistic mindset you want to be in. Repeating them before you go to bed can help you to wrap the day up in a very pleasant way too. Really, though, you can use affirmations any time of the day (Mind Tools Content Team, n.d.). This goes double for anytime you're faced with a tough situation and are struggling with negative thoughts and emotions despite your best efforts. Affirmations can be really useful for recalibrating your mind in moments like that and thus, attracting the kinds of positive things you want in life rather than the negative things your thoughts might otherwise steer you toward.

How do you write a love affirmation, then? You get started by thinking carefully about what it is you want when it comes to love. What kind of relationship do you want to have? What do you need from your partner? Is it emotional support? Someone you'll feel safe with? Someone you feel free to goof off and have fun with? Whatever the case may be, writing an affirmation begins with deciding what it is you want and need. Having done that, you can get to work turning the thing you want or need into a positive affirmation. Interestingly enough, those negative thoughts you had recorded in your notebook can come in handy at this juncture. You can use them to craft positive thoughts, which you can then use as daily affirmations. The golden rule to remember here is to write your affirmation in the present tense and, obviously, to make sure that it is something positive.

The final rule to remember about affirmations is that you need to say them with feeling, like you fully and completely believe in what you are saying. This way, your affirmation will carry more of an emotional weight and your brain will be even more likely to take them as absolutely undeniable facts. If you are confused as to what love affirmations might look like, here are couple of examples for you to consider:

- I am letting love into my life.
- I am worthy and deserving of loving and of being loved.
- I deserve to have a truly fulfilling relationship.
- I am a unique, interesting, and wonderful human being.
- I love myself.
- I am attracting trusting, caring, and loving relationships into my life.

Manifestation, in part, is all about acting as though you already have that which you want. This is something that works particularly well in combination with positive affirmations and positive self-talk. Acting like you already have what you want is a technique that is better known as "act as if" (Louise, 2020). Act-as-if is built on the idea that manifesting is not just about thinking of the things you want. It is also about acting on them. Thoughts that are not followed up with actions ultimately do not yield results. Say that you met the perfect partner, someone who can really love you and that you can truly fall in love with. They texted you the very next day wanting to get together for coffee. How likely is it that you'll end up in a relationship with this person if you never reply to their texts? Not very likely, of course.

Taking action, then, is a very important part of manifestation but only so long as you take the right kind of action, which is exactly what act-as-if is. Act-as-if, however, is not the same thing as faking it until you make it. Faking it till you make it entails pretending you already have everything that you want. Acting-as-if, on the other hand, entails doing things that are outside of your comfort zone so that you can embody and attract the kind of energy you want in your life. In practice, act-as-if unfolds in three phases. Phase one is all about self-awareness, as it requires that you become cognizant of your emotions and your thoughts. After all, you can't change your thoughts and emotions, or the behaviors and attitudes that they fuel if you're not aware of them.

If self-awareness is something that you struggle with, then journaling is something you may want to try out. Journaling is a proven way of improving your self-awareness levels, seeing as it allows you to explore your thoughts and feelings in depth and get to the root causes that lie at their very core. When you journal regularly, you start noticing behavioral patterns and you can't help but analyze them further. Over time, you gain a thorough understanding of why you do some of the things that you do. If you're trying out journaling as part of your journey to manifest love, then you are going to have to question your outlook and approach to love. For instance, you may want to ask yourself what, exactly, is holding you back from manifesting love. You may further want to question what your biggest fears are when it comes to love. Is it the idea of being vulnerable with someone else and thus of getting hurt? Is it losing the person that you love? Is it something else entirely?

By asking yourself such questions during your journaling exercise, you can come to really grasp what you think and feel about love itself, as well as your ability to accept love. That done, you can move onto phase two, which is about aligning the actions you take with your wants and desires. The easiest way to accomplish this is to pretend it is not you that has this desire but someone else. So, ask yourself how someone who desires a healthy relationship or a fulfilling kind of love acts. Be honest and thorough in your answers. Then, do your best to act in that way so that you can manifest love. If you said that a person who desires a fulfilling kind of love acts in a more emotionally open and vulnerable way, then perhaps acting like that is a good idea. You do not have to make any dramatic changes right off the bat, of course, especially since you're unused to acting like that. You can start small, like with a small group of trusted people. Once you've been doing that a while, you can slowly expand your circle, so that you're more emotionally available to others as well. Over time, you'll be able to lower your guard a bit more with new people too, thereby inviting love into your life.

Acting-as-if can affect anything from the way you speak and to the way you present yourself to others. It can influence how you spend your time and with who, as well as how you treat the people around you. As an extension of that, it can impact how you show up for others and how you make decisions on a day-to-day basis. In adjusting to these different things you inevitably arrive at phase three, which is letting go. The main thing you need to let go of to manifest love—or anything else—is the feeling that you need to or should do something. This is admittedly difficult to do, but it is immensely necessary. When you get hung up on the things you need, you focus more on what you "should" or "shouldn't" be doing, rather than on what you want. This proves to be a limitation in the long run. Hence, it prevents you from acting-as-if.

Being able to let go of "need" requires placing your trust in the universe. It means recognizing that your desires are in alignment with universal energy, which will deliver them right to it, if only you'd let it (Alex, 2020). Trusting the universe necessitates relinquishing your sense of control a bit, which is why this can be hard to do, at least for some of us. The reason why it is necessary is simple: You do not exactly know how the universe is going to deliver what you want to you nor even when it will do so. It is not possible for you to do so, really. That means there are two things you can do. You can either try to control things in vain and hold yourself back from acting-as-if or you can take a deep breath, remind yourself that you trust the universe, and continue on your way.

Taking Action

Having spoken some about the importance of taking the "right" kind of actions, we would be remiss not to touch upon the kinds of actions you ought to avoid. A lot of people operate on the misconception that you cannot say no to any new opportunities if you want to manifest the things you want. This, however, is incorrect. The truth is that you'll actually be able to manifest your disease better by eliminating the things that you do not want from your life. This can equal eliminating any number of things from toxic people to events and places you simply do not want to go to or behaviors that do not serve you but do hinder you.

Saying no to such things when you need to is vital because it is both empowering and liberating. A lot of the time, we end up saying yes to things that we simply do not want to do because we find it hard to say "no" to others. We find it equally hard to draw boundaries between ourselves and other people. In doing so, we end up putting other people's needs and wants above our own, much to our detriment. This not only damages our emotional, physical, and mental well-being by draining us, but keeps us from behaving in a way that would actually attract the things we want our way. Learning to say "no", then, requires putting yourself first and saying "yes" to your needs and wants, first and foremost (Laura Raduenz, 2020). The great thing about learning to say "no" when we need to is that it makes it easier for you to accept responsibility for the things you want. It makes you acknowledge that manifesting the things you want is on you. No one else is going to do it for you and the universe will only deliver the things you want if you put the right energy out there and start acting-as-if.

If you are new to the art of saying "no", the first thing you need to do is identify the right opportunity to do so. Is someone asking you to do something that technically you can do, but that will cause you to exhaust and drain yourself in the long run? Then you probably should say no, since your needs and well-being are just as important as those of others. Is someone asking you to do something and you do not want to but are worried that you'll disappoint that person? Again, this is a good and valid opportunity to say no. As tempted as you may feel, the fear of disappointing others is not a good enough reason to agree to something, especially since you are not responsible for anyone's feelings except for your own.

Identifying the right opportunities to say no to others is just the beginning, though. After that, you have to actually say the word. If this is a struggle for you, then one thing you could do is practice saying no, in front of a mirror and everything. You might feel a little silly for a moment, but that feeling will soon go away. After that, you'll be left with the expression on your face as you say "no", the tone of voice you say it in—for the record it should be kind yet firm—and the words you use. The more you practice these things, the easier they will become and the more natural they will come to feel. This is something you'll truly appreciate when you actually have to say "no" to someone outside of your practice sessions. Thanks to your rehearsals, so to speak, you'll be able to draw your boundaries more calmly and without rushing or rambling. Thus, you'll get to both look out for your well-being and ensure that your actions become more aligned with the things you want to manifest.

Sustaining Manifestation

By now, it should be abundantly clear that manifestation is part and parcel with a positive mindset. Hence, the more you can do to maintain a positive mindset, the easier manifesting love will become for you. This is why things like positive affirmations and positive self-talk are important, as you have. Positive thinking techniques like this often begin with self-awareness, which is a concept many of us struggle with. Becoming more aware of your thoughts and feelings amidst the fifty million other responsibilities you have to juggle on a day to day basis would be hard for anyone (Muse Team, 2023). There are things you can do to get better at this, though, and chief among them is practicing mindfulness. How could that not be the case when self-awareness is the very foundation mindfulness is built on?

Mindfulness is essentially a state of consciousness where self-awareness is wedded to your attention and focus. It is something that allows you to be fully present in a given moment, noticing and observing everything, including your own emotions and thoughts, without remotely judging them (Lippincott, 2017). One of the best possible ways you can increase your level of self-awareness is by regularly doing mindfulness meditations. There are two kinds of mindfulness meditations you can do if you're interested: One involving focusing on an object and one without any kind of object to focus on (*Meditation for Awareness*, 2021).

Both meditations start out the same way. You sit down in a comfortable place and position and start breathing in and out slowly and deeply. If you're meditating with an object—for argument's sake, let us say it is a vase—then you keep your eyes trained on it. As you meditate you try to take notice of everything there is to notice about that vase. What is its shape and color like? How does its texture look? How tall or short is the vase and where does its shadow fall? Is its surface chipped or smooth? By keeping your attention fixed on the vase, you focus and root it in the present moment. In doing so, you gradually improve your ability to remain in the moment and with it, your levels of self-awareness.

As for meditation without an object, this entails doing more or less the same thing with two key differences. The first is that with this type of meditation you are allowed to close your eyes, so long as you do not fall asleep. The second is that you focus not on a vase, but everything you can feel in that moment. This includes the feel of the couch cushion beneath you and the ground beneath your feet. It also includes the temperature of the room, the sounds you can hear around you, the various sensations going through your body, and the thoughts flitting in and out of your mind. The idea here is to notice the thoughts you have but not to chase after them. If you find yourself getting stuck in a certain line of thought, what you should do is gently—and without chastising yourself—bring your attention back to the present moment. This will be tough at first, as our minds are not very used to letting go of thoughts. As with many other things we have covered in this chapter, though, it will get easier and easier to do the more often you practice it. That means that you should be practicing this every day if you are able to. Mindfulness meditation can only increase your levels of self-awareness if you turn it into a regular habit.

Since meditation can be a tough habit to develop—let us face it, most of us find it hard to sit still doing apparently "nothing—you may find it rather challenging. One thing that might make things easier on you is to keep your initial meditation sessions only a minute or so long. Once you have gotten used to that, you can extend the amount of time you spend meditation to three minutes, and then to five, and so on and so forth. Before you know it, you'll find that you are able to meditate for a good 20, even 30 minutes in one sitting. You'll also find that your meditation practice has increased your ability to recognize and understand your own feelings, which you absolutely need to do if you are to manifest love. I mean, how can you draw the right energies to yourself if you're not able to recognize what kind of energies you're sending out into the universe?

Naturally, the kinds of emotions you feel and put out there do not just affect your ability to manifest love. It impacts how well you are able to manifest other things like wealth. You would be very surprised, in fact, to hear just how large a role feelings like generosity and gratitude can play in your ability to manifest wealth, as you'll find out in the coming chapter.

Chapter 3:
Manifesting Wealth

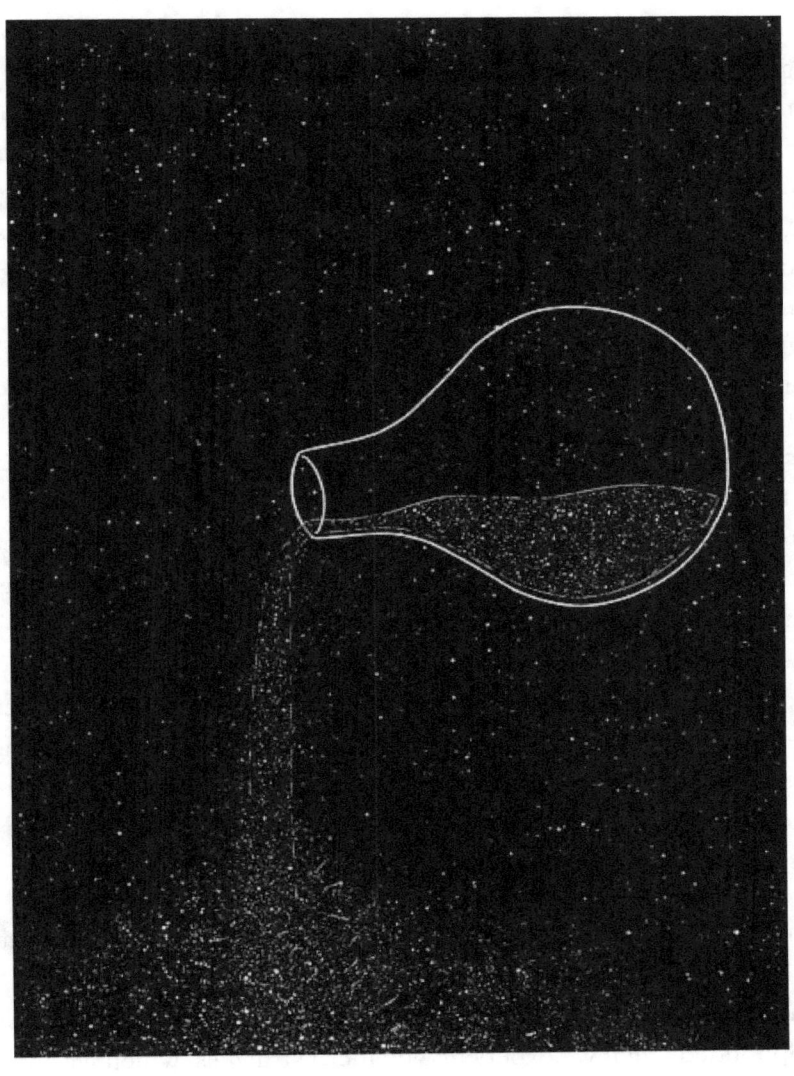

Fortune sides with him who dares. –Virgil

One of the chief things any person wants to manifest in life is wealth. Wealth can be defined as the overall assets that you are in possession of. In other words, it indicates how much money and other monetary assets you have (The Investopedia Team, 2019). This might sound a bit trivial to some, but let us face it, we all want to be able to manifest wealth, given the kind of world that we live in. Manifesting wealth is something that would allow you to live a more comfortable, even luxurious life, after all. Yet despite this and despite how hard we all work on a day-to-day basis, a significant number of us have a very poor relationship with money— pun intended. They struggle with manifesting wealth, in fact, to the point where monetary concerns and the quest for financial stability become a regular part of their lives. The primary thing that a lot of these people forget is that while wealth does have a lot to do with work, it has just as much to do with your mindset and the belief system you've woven around it. This is a shame because the truth is by changing these two things, you actually can change your relationship with money and thus, your ability to manifest the wealth you want.

If you want to change your relationship with money and manifest wealth, the first thing you need to do is figure out what kind of relationship you currently have with it (Canfield, 2019). What are your existing and— crucially—limiting beliefs about money? How do these beliefs impact your dealing with money and your ability to manifest wealth? The limiting beliefs you have about money most likely come from your childhood. They are beliefs that you've grown up with and have taken to accepting as undeniable and irrevocable truths when they are nothing of the sort. Before you can even think about manifesting wealth, you need to identify what your limiting beliefs about money are and actively dismantle them.

Most limiting beliefs about money are rooted in fear. There is the fear of not having enough, the fear of losing what you have, the fear of not being able to manage your money well… These fears are often compounded when we experience financial struggles, which we all do at one point or another, even if it is for the briefest of moments. The problem with this is that not only do these beliefs put out the wrong kind of energy into the world, thus stopping you from manifesting, they also filter into your subconscious. The reason why that is problematic is that your subconscious mind plays a huge role in your decision making processes. Studies show that your subconscious mind takes less than 10 seconds to make a decision without you ever realizing it and, yes, that includes financial decisions (*Case Closed for Free Will?*, 2008). Factor in the fact that your subconscious mind is responsible for 95% of all the decisions you make and it is clear to see how your fear-based limiting beliefs about money can affect your relationship with wealth and your ability to manifest it.

If you want to dismantle your limiting beliefs about money, you must first become aware of them. Luckily, there are various signs you can pay attention to that indicate you hold onto such beliefs. One is a feeling of shame, guilt, or fear that spikes whenever you spend any money, even you have more than enough in the bank (Katrina, 2021). Other signs include:

- getting stuck in a perpetual loop of famine and feast
- feeling certain that you'll never be able to make enough money
- thinking of money as a limited resource
- feeling envious, jealous, upset, or angry when you see something that you want
- being afraid of there being an expensive emergency, like a medical emergency, that you'll have to take care of
- falling for get-rich-quick schemes
- buying things you don't really need or want just in case or just because they are on a discount
- being afraid to make money because that means you'll have to pay more in taxes

- not setting big financial goals for yourself because you're afraid you'll not be able to achieve them

- hoarding money but never really spending it on anything you want or that is fun to do

- spending more money that you actually have to impress someone (no, this does not count as "acting-as-if" as you'll see later)

- not throwing things away even when you never use them because you think you might need them someday

- feeling upset or even outraged at the thought of sharing your wealth with someone

- avoiding looking at your bank account or refusing to keep track of your finances because it will make you stressed and anxious (which is a poor financial habit to have, as you'll, again, see later)

- saying that you can't afford something and thus refraining from buying it, even when you can afford it

That such beliefs, thoughts, and behaviors put out negative energy regarding wealth into the universe is evident That you need to get to work fixing these beliefs is even more so. So, then, how do you do that? Again, you first identify which limiting beliefs you have. You can use the signs listed here as a means of doing that but you can also question things like how you feel when you look at your bank account or when you see something you want that happens to be pricey. Asking yourself what you're afraid of if you were to become wealthy, or what your relationship with money is like, and whether there are any patterns you can discern there should help too. One of the most important questions you can ask yourself is whether you feel deserving of money. If you feel undeserving of wealth, after all, you neither will be able to put in the effort required to accumulate it nor will you be able to manifest it using the law of attraction.

To dismantle your limiting beliefs about wealth, you have to work on changing your perspective on wealth and money. A great way of doing this is to write down the limiting beliefs you've identified, then try to write down the exact opposite, freeing version of it. This exercise is similar, if you'll notice, to changing our negative self-talk into positive self-talk. So much so that it can be considered a version of it. So, say that one of your limiting beliefs is "I'll never be able to make that much money." The more positive and freeing version of this sentence might be, "I can make as much money as I need, so long as I put in the effort and work smart." If that makes sense, here are a couple of limiting belief transformations that you can try your hand at

Limiting Belief	Freeing belief
I am not deserving of wealth.	
This is far too expensive for me.	
What if I can't earn any more after this?	
I am really not good at handling my finances.	

Since turning limiting beliefs into freeing beliefs is very similar to turning negative self-talk into positive self-talk, one way you could get even better at converting one into the other is to try to notice how you talk to other people about money. The same can be said about making a conscious effort to notice how you act where money and financial matters are concerned. The more you notice such things, the more you'll be able to pick up on your limiting and problematic words and behaviors. When you are looking at these different behaviors, a part of your mind might pipe up and say that some of them are not all that bad. Say that you have a habit of hoarding money just in case you have an emergency of some sort. You might think this is a good habit. The thing is, though, when you hoard money in case of emergencies or disasters, you end up attracting and even subconsciously seeking them out.

So, what if you did not call your savings account your "in case of emergency fund" or "your rainy day stash"? What if you called it something more positive, like "the feel good fund" or "the extra sunny day stash"? This kind of thing might seem like it is too simple a solution to change your perspective on wealth. Often, however, the simplest of solutions are the most effective ones and this is the case right here. Giving your savings account a positive name with positive connotations generates a lot of good feelings. This helps to attract good things your way, like more wealth and great opportunities to spend some of yours on.

The key to changing your limiting beliefs, then, is to ask yourself how you can learn to look at matters differently, where wealth is concerned. It might take you a while to arrive at the right answer but that is alright. While you work on that, you can always try these exercises that we have covered and thus, put the law of attraction to excellent use.

Why Getting Comfortable With Spending Money is Important

Here is something that might sound a little paradoxical to you: If you want to generate and hold onto wealth, then you need to actually spend some of your money. This might sound counterintuitive or counterproductive to some, especially those use to hoarding money for a "rainy day" but it is true. A lot of us are hesitant to spend money but such hesitancy is another kind of limiting belief. It even has a name: Money guilt. While anyone can have money guilt, the people that experience it the most are those individuals that have struggled financially in the past, particularly when they were young. Such people usually have what we call a scarcity mindset and it is this mindset you need to shift out of if you want to manifest wealth (Yuille, 2021).

If you struggle with money guilt, then odds are your scarcity mindset becomes triggered when you have to spend it on something other than what could be considered a necessity, such as food. To overcome this, you must make a decent financial plan—which you'll learn how to do shortly—that takes care of your basic needs and responsibilities first. Once those bases are covered, your guilt should be alleviated to some degree.

The next thing you'll need to do is to keep track of your finances. People who have money guilt often prefer not to look at their bank accounts or track their finances. This is because seeing how much money they have been spending immediately makes them feel guilty and anxious. This is problematic, though, because when you don't track your finances, you lose the ability to assure yourself that you're fulfilling all your responsibilities and the ability to plan your spending wisely. Once you've taken a look at your finances and covered your responsibilities, you'll want to move onto determining your main source of guilt. What kind of expenditure makes you feel the most guilty? What kind of situations cause your money guilt to spike? Is it possible, for instance, that you're comparing your financial situation to that of others or is it more that spending money on certain things like a trip, or clothes, makes you feel more guilty?

Truthfully, identifying the source of your guilt is the only way you can ever get rid of money guilt. One thing you can do when you are faced with these triggers is to remind yourself that you've already taken care of all your responsibilities and are therefore not doing anything wrong. Another is to use the 30-day saving rule. The 30-day saving rule dictates that you have to wait 30 days to purchase something you really want, like a new bottle of perfume or the new PS5, for example. If you still want that item after 30 days have gone by, then you can get it. If your desire for it has waned, however, you can skip it and save your money for something you'll truly want. The 30-day saving rule is a great strategy to adopt both because it can help you to manage your finances well and because it can do away with unnecessary guilt. It can keep you from making impulse buys that you'll come to regret later and allow you to actually feel good about yourself when you do treat yourself to something once the 30 day period is up (Diehl, 2022).

A final, phenomenal way of shifting out of the scarcity mindset and getting comfortable with spending money is to assign value to it. Manifesting wealth—or anything else for that matter—is all about setting intentions. By setting an intention to the various different purchases that you make, you can start changing the inner dialogue you've about how you spend your money. (Financial Gym Team, 2021) In the process, you can change your entire relationship with it. Let us say that you're treating yourself to a spa day but you feel guilty about it. A massage can be rather expensive, after all. You can consider this purchase unnecessary, in which case your guilt will climb rather than go away and you'll find that you're unable to relax at all. Alternatively, you can tell yourself that this is something you are doing for your physical and mental health, after working so hard for so long.

In setting this intent on this purchase, you'll reaffirm how important your well-being is. You'll add value to your purchase and remind yourself of your own value and both these things will decrease your guilt and anxiety about spending money significantly. You'll increase your happiness and relaxation levels and draw more relaxing, satisfying things your way. You'll even be able to come to see your purchase as something necessary, rather than a superfluous thing.

Assigning value to your purchases is something you can do with anything and everything you spend money on. If you are renting or purchasing a new apartment that is pricier than your old place, for example, you can remind yourself that you're doing this for your safety and comfort, which are very important. Likewise, if you are splurging on a fancy dinner with some friends, you can remind yourself that you're doing this to make good memories with your valued friends and show them that you care about them. How long could a friendship last, after all, if you don't spend any time with the person before you?

The most important thing about assigning value to your purchases is that it changes your understanding on why you are working to make money in the first place. It makes your relationship with money a whole lot more positive. As such, it makes earning money into something more pleasant, uplifting, maybe even fun, rather than a worrisome, stress-inducing task you have to do to survive. This outlook puts out a lot of positive energy regarding money, which inevitably draws more of it your way.

Putting Yourself Into Abundant Environments

The beauty of the law of attraction is that it can be used in a multitude of different ways. You can use it, for example, by thinking positively and more often about the things you want, thereby drawing them to you. You can also use it by putting yourself in environments that are bursting with the very things that you want to manifest. If you were to do both of these things at the same time, you'd actually make it easier for the law of attraction to work, since that which you want would be closer to you than before in this case. This is why putting yourself into abundant environments is important for manifesting wealth.

One of the greatest benefits that putting yourself into abundant environments has to offer you is that it actively counters a scarcity mindset. It supports your efforts to cultivate an abundance mindset instead. Putting yourself in abundant environments can mean a variety of things. Going for a walk in a very well-off part of town would be one example. Another might be to attend a networking event in your industry that you know will be attended by very wealthy people. Still another might be to peruse high end stores, even if you'll not be purchasing anything just then.

Immersing yourself in an abundant environment does not just mean doing large things like these though. Something as simple as treating yourself to a fancy cup of coffee every once in a while or buying ingredients at the slightly fancier grocery store for a change, instead of your usual one would count as well. These changes, while small, can invite more wealth into your life by allowing you to put out the right energy for it—so long as you do it without feeling guilty about it immediately afterward, of course. Now, all this does not mean you should spend money like water and get cup after cup of artisan coffee every day. But allowing yourself to splurge in this way and surrounding yourself with the people, things, events that scream abundance is one of the surest ways of attracting wealth.

Manifesting wealth by immersing yourself in abundance works best when it is done with gratitude. In fact, manifesting wealth typically gets easier when you make a point to practice gratitude every day. Expressing gratitude means giving genuine thanks and appreciation for the wealth you already have. When you don't acknowledge your gratitude and show it, you block the positive energies you send out. As a result, you limit the flow of wealth and abundance in your life. You achieve the exact opposite of this, however, when you take a moment to pause and allow yourself to feel gratitude for everything you have in your life. This practice recalibrates the energy you are sending out, ensuring that it is the exact right vibrational frequency you want it to be.

The best and possibly easiest way to practice gratitude is keeping a gratitude journal. There is no right or wrong way to go about keeping such a journal, so long as you make sure to write in it every day for just 10 to 15 minutes (*Gratitude Journal*, 2018). Whatever you record in your gratitude journal is up to you, of course. Examples of some things you could give thanks for in it might be having a safe and warm roof over your head or being able to make a living and take care of yourself and your family. Alternatively, you might record good things that have happened to you that day. For instance, if you splurged just a bit on a spa day or to get a really good friend a great gift for their 30th birthday, then writing about it and showing gratitude for your ability to do these things is a great idea. You can write about the things that you're grateful for either using a list format or you can get as descriptive and long winded about them as you'd like. This is not a college essay after all and no one is going to check your grammar and syntax.

The beauty of gratitude journals is that they often make you realize that you have a lot more to be grateful about than you thought. This naturally uplifts your mood, fuels your positive thinking habits, and strengthens your ability to cultivate an abundance mindset. One thing you can try to take all this a step further and really get use your manifestation powers is to give thanks in your journal for the things you want to manifest. The trick here is to write in the present tense as if you already have what you want, as sort of an extension of the acting-as-if technique. It is also to be as specific about what you are grateful for, be it something you have or something you'll get in the future. While you're at it, you may want to try to get as detailed and personal about things as you can. This way, you can really start seeing how many different things you have in your life that are worthy of your appreciation.

As a final note, you might want to get into the habit of considering or defining the things you are expressing your gratitude for as gifts. Like labeling your savings account the "really sunny day fund", this can improve your outlook on your life and the things you have significantly and keep you from taking things for granted.

Visualizing Wealth

Visualization is one of the most useful and effective mental tools in your manifestation toolkits, as you know. It stands to reason, then, that visualizing wealth is a phenomenal way of manifesting it. As with love, there are a couple of different ways you can visualize wealth. The first thing you need to do is to decide what you want to manifest your wealth for. Is it that you really want to go on a trip and need money for it or that you want to save up more money in general? Is it that you want to be able to get your parents a fantastic anniversary gift or splurge on yourself?

Once you have clarity on what you want to achieve, you can focus on visualizing the wealth needed for it. Let us say that you are trying to manifest the wealth you need for a coat that you really want. You have waited 30 days before getting that coat and your desire for it has not waned. One thing you can do to manifest in this case is to imagine yourself wearing that coat in your everyday life. Alternatively, let us say that it is not an object that you're trying to manifest but a promotion or a bonus at work. The visualization strategy to employ here is to imagine yourself—as vividly as possible, remember—getting these things that you want.

What if it is wealth in general that you want to manifest? In this case, you could envision yourself looking at your bank account and watching those numbers climb. Another, more physical exercise you can do at this point is to write yourself a check for the money you want to have. This is a proven method of manifesting wealth, if Jim Carrey's—of all people—story about it is anything to go by. Before Jim Carrey became a famous Hollywood star, he was an unknown actor struggling to find work. He was also—and still is—a great believer in manifestation and the law of attraction. So, he would visualize himself being given various roles by different directors all the time. One day, Carrey took out his checkbook and wrote himself a check for $10 million for "acting services rendered" (Dhruv Bose, 2022). He then gave himself five years to earn that money. At the time, he did not have any promising leads, acting-wise. So it was that the years started ticking by until one day Carrey at last caught a break. The year was 1995 and the part he was offered was in the movie Dumb & Dumber. This was to be his first major role and the check he was given for? It was exactly $10 million.

Jim Carrey's story is probably one of the clearest examples as to how effective manifestation can be in getting you the things you want. So, if you want to manifest wealth, writing yourself a check could be a very effective visualization technique to try. So could creating a vision journal. A vision journal is a weekly journal that you write in to gain better clarity on your future financial goals. You can physically write in this journal or treat it as the notebook version of a vision board and fill its pages with images you've printed out or cut out of magazines to represent your goals.   You can do both at the same time too.

If you're going to be writing in your journal, you may want to explore things like what you want your life to look like five or ten years from now (Takhar, n.d.). You may want to reflect on the things you have at this present moment, as well as the things you can express your gratitude for. While you're doing that, you could pepper your journal with the images and visuals you find symbolizing the financial goals you want to meet. As you go through your journal, you'll notice that your vision for the future becomes more and more detailed and easier to see with each entry. You'll further notice that your behavior in your day-to-day life is changing so that it becomes aligned with the things you want. Most interestingly, though, after enough time has gone by, you'll see that the goals and desires you've been writing about in your journal have started to come to fruition.

Goal Setting

Vision journals center around your ability to set financial goals for yourself, as you can see. Goal setting is important in manifestation because it allows you to gain clarity on what, exactly, you want to achieve or get, set an intention, and act on that intention. Put another way, goal setting makes it easier for you to take the actions you need to manifest what you want. This is important because manifestation without action is meaningless, for the most part. Think about it this way: Would Jim Carrey have been cast in *Dumb & Dumber* and would he have gotten that $10 million check if he had not gone to casting calls? Of course he would not have. Instead, he would have remained undiscovered and would never have gotten to become the star he dreamed of being.

The thing about taking action for the things that you want is that you sometimes don't know what action you are supposed to take. This is where good goal setting skills can help you. Good goal setting skills can help you figure out exactly what you need to do to get what you want and break it down into small, sensible steps. These skills begin with something called SMART goals, which stands for:

Specific

Measurable

Achievable

Relevant

Time-bound

A specific goal is one that is as clearly defined and narrow in scope as possible. It is important that your goals be specific as opposed to vague for two reasons. The first is that specific goals are easier to meet as they tell you exactly what you need to do to achieve them (Herrity, 2019). The second is that specific goals send a more specific, clearly felt energy out into the universe and help you to manifest quicker. A measurable goal, meanwhile, is one where you can track your progress. When a goal is not measurable, you have trouble with this and sometimes feel as though you're not making any kind of headway. This rapidly drains any motivation you might have, making you less likely to keep going. The less motivated you become, the more negative energy you put out into the world, making it more difficult to manifest the wealth you want.

When you set measurable goals, though, the exact opposite happens. Pretty soon, you are meeting milestone after milestone with no signs of stopping.

For a goal to be achievable, it has to be something that is actually in the realm of possibility. As an example, you probably will not be able to go from having a couple of grand in your bank account to having millions in the span of a month, at least not unless you win the lottery or a rich uncle you didn't know existed leaves you a grand inheritance, like something out of a movie. So, if you set this kind of goal for yourself, you're probably not going to be able to meet it. However, if you set an achievable goal for yourself, you'll be able to craft a game plan to get exactly what you want and then get to work. Thus, you'll be able to meet your financial goals with ease. Not only that, but because you know your goal is within the realm of possibility, you'll end up believing in it more, thereby adding fuel to your manifestation powers.

As for relevance, this simply means that the goals that you set for yourself should ultimately align with both your long term goals and your personal values. Otherwise, the resultant crash is going to make it impossible for you to meet your goals. Your inability to meet your goals will further dishearten you and even keep you from trying again with different, SMARTer goals. Finally, goals have to be time-bound. That means that the goals you need to set for yourself need to be achievable in a predetermined period of time. This increases your goals' specificity, you see, making them more tangible, making you believe in your ability to meet them, and making you work in a more strategic way to achieve them in time.

On the whole, there are three kinds of financial goals you can set for yourself. These are process goals, result goals, and breakthrough goals (Fox, n.d.). Process goals are the most short-term goals you can set for yourself. Setting short term goals is important because such goals outline the daily and weekly actions you have taken to achieve your most major—meaning breakthrough—goals. Say that you want to be a millionaire (yes, that is a vague goal, but go with it for now). What are the short term goals you need to set to do this? What actions do you need to take every day, so that your efforts will build on top of one another and carry you toward your actual goal?

What makes setting short term goals incredibly effective where manifestation is concerned is that they boost your energy, motivation, and satisfaction levels every time you achieve them. That sends all the right kinds of energy out into the universe, carrying you onward and bringing your wants and desires one step closer to you with each passing day.

Just as there are short term goals you can set for yourself there are bigger, long-term goals. These goals are still steps you need to take to meet your most major goal though. Say that your breakthrough goal is to become the CEO of your company. That is a very long term goal because before you can become a CEO you need to first be promoted to manager, then branch manager, and so on and so forth. On the one hand, those promotions are goals that will take you a while to achieve. Hence, they are long term goals. On the other hand, they are steps you need to take to achieve your ultimate goal, which means that they too are milestones you need to pass to get what you want.

Breakthrough goals, meanwhile, are goals that are big enough to be outside of your present reality and possibilities. They are things that are possible to achieve and get in the future, but not at this particular moment. As such, they require you to put in some degree of work and effort over an extended period of time. Keeping your spirits high and retaining a positive mindset in pursuit of breakthrough goals can be challenging at times, but this is why process goals and result goals are so important. So, how do you set them? How do you set the kinds of goals that will help you to manifest the very things that you want?

Start by writing down your breakthrough goal first. Make it as SMART as humanly possible. Then start thinking about the things you need to achieve in the short, medium, and long terms to achieve it. Write these down. Try to write and define every single step you'd need to take to meet these various goals. Those steps will be your process goals and again, they will need to be SMART. As you are writing down your goals, make sure you use the present tense (Rosenberg McKay, 2022). That way you can bring manifestation into things more. Acting-as-if and talking as though you already have something are effective manifestation techniques, as you'll recall, and they can easily be made a part of manifestation.

Another important rule to follow when goal setting is to always use positive language. For instance, you should never talk about the things you don't want. Instead, they should focus on what you want and need (Sturm, 2019). This way, you can be sure you're using your positive thinking skills when expressing your goals, as opposed to negative thinking, which is bound by limited beliefs. Another thing you can do when setting goals is to use active language. The goals you set for yourself can be either active or passive. Passive goals all express things that you want to be or get. They are things that happen to you, not things you actively pursue. Active goals, on the other hand, focus on what you can and want to do. They use action verbs, thus showing you what you need to do to achieve success. They make you believe more in your ability to achieve your goals by putting the burden of responsibility on you, as opposed to outside forces. They make you feel more positive about your efforts, which kicks the law of attraction to overdrive.

One thing to keep in mind about goal setting is that they should always be flexible, regardless of whether they are long term or short term. No matter what kind of goals you set, you're going to encounter certain obstacles along the way (Rosenberg McKay, 2022). When that happens, you need to hold onto your positive mindset and adjust your goals accordingly, rather than giving up. If meeting a certain financial goal is taking you longer than anticipated, for example, then maybe what you need to do is adjust the timeline for your goal. This requires flexibility on your part and it is crucial to manifestation, the law of attraction, and you achieving everything you want. Once you've adjusted your plans, you'll have to roll up your sleeves and get to work because—again—manifestation only really works so long as you follow it up with the right behaviors and actions. Then, what actions do you have to take—aside from those outlined in your goals, of course—manifest the wealth you want?

Budgeting For Manifesting Wealth

You have already seen that there are several things you can do to manifest wealth, like putting yourself into abundant environments and setting goals. But there are smaller, yet no less important things you can do too. The first of these is learning how to budget. For the record, budgeting does not mean not splurging on something when you really want it. You can definitely do this, so long as you remember the 30 day rule. It may even be beneficial that you do this from time to time since this can help you to attract more wealth. The key words in that sentence are "from time to time" because manifesting wealth requires being able to hold onto some of the money that you make. Budgeting can help you to do that, while still allowing you to spend your money without feeling guilty about it.

Budgeting often seems like one of those impossible tasks to take on but it is actually a lot easier than you'd think. This is thanks to the 50-30-20 rule. The 50-30-20 rule is pretty simple (O'Shea & Schwahn, 2021) It says that you're supposed to:

- use 50% of what you earn to cover your basic needs, like groceries, bills, and rent

- use 30% of your income for the things you want

- save 20% of your income or use it to pay off any debts you have

The 50-30-20 rule is as simple as that. Not only is it very simple but it is also quite effective. That is why it is an immensely popular budgeting method that helps you to maximize the amount of money you save while making sure all your needs and a big majority of your wants are covered. Budgeting is good for manifesting wealth because, aside from the obvious—making it possible for you to grow your savings—it makes you feel a lot more in control and relaxed where your finances are concerned. It reaffirms your sense of security, making it possible for you to spend your money without feeling guilty about it. It makes you feel more in control and increases your trust in the wealth that is to come your way in the future. This inevitably brings more wealth your way, making you even more comfortable, able to meet your financial goals, and financially secure.

Put simply, then, the very act of budgeting can support your ability to manifest wealth in a myriad of different ways. It can even support your ability to manifest abundance, which is not the same thing as wealth, though it is related to it, as you'll come to discover in the next chapter.

Chapter 4:

Manifesting Abundance

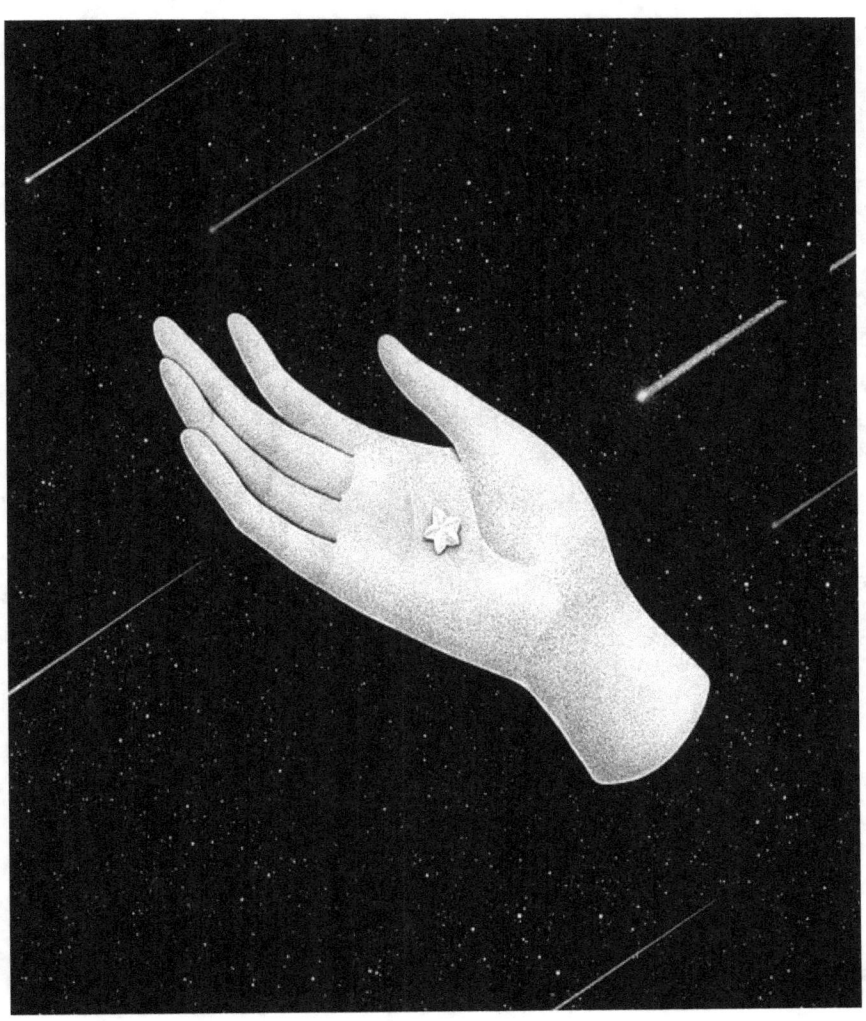

Abundance is not something we acquire, it is something we tune into. –Wayne Dyer

A lot of us tend to mistake abundance for wealth. This makes an abundance of sense, seeing as the two concepts are intimately related. What makes wealth different from abundance is that it is an end state. It is an endpoint that you want to get to and remain at (Maxwell, 2018). Abundance, on the other hand, is your ability to generate "something" in ample quantities. That something can be "money" and "wealth", of course, but it does not necessarily have to be. Abundance can easily refer to the friends and good relationships you have in your life or any other kind of blessing. To put it very simply, abundance is your ability to grow, manifest, and to have and become more than what you have and more than what you are (Sasson, 2020). It is your tendency to create and produce more of everything and it is a tendency that we all have. It is just not a habit that we all cultivate, even though we should.

Your ability to manifest abundance is deeply entrenched in the faith and belief that you have in yourself and your abilities (Mandel, 2021). It is your belief in these things that fuels the effort you put into getting the things that you want and the patience you show in pursuit of them. It is this belief that motivates you to keep going even when you face difficulties and hold onto a positive mindset. The belief you have in yourself is just the first component of your ability to manifest abundance, then. There are three others: Effort, process, and perseverance. If you want to manifest abundance, it is these four components that you need to work on.

Your Beliefs and Your Desires

Whether you're able to manifest abundance has a lot to do with how much you believe in yourself and what you believe about the world. Obviously, you'll not be able to manifest much of anything if you don't ultimately believe that you'll be able to. You also will not be able to manifest abundance if you don't inherently believe in the limitlessness of the world. Most people believe one of three things about the world: that there is never enough for everyone that is living in it, that the world has just enough to offer to everybody, and that the world has more than enough to offer to all. Which of these beliefs you hold onto plays a crucial role in manifesting abundance (Meltzer, 2018).

If you were to take these belief systems one by one, you'd easily be able to see which are more in keeping with an optimistic mindset and which are decidedly not. Believing that the world does not have enough to offer to everyone that is living in it clearly possesses a more negative mindset, for example. This kind of belief paints a very negative picture of the world in and of itself. How could it not when the people that hold to this belief clearly only see the things that they lack and not the blessings that they have? People who belong to this school of thought tend to have limited worldviews. They seldom express gratitude and take the things that they have for granted, until they lose them, that is. They see the world as a dog-eat-dog kind of place. They believe that there are only a finite amount of resources for everyone out there and someone always has to lose in order for them to win.

As you might have guessed, this is limiting belief in and of itself, as it is very fear based. The fear here is an obvious one: What if I don't get what I want? Living your life holding onto a belief system that is built on such a fear sends out the wrong energy out into the universe, of course. By the rules of the law of attraction, this works against a person's interest, blocking them from getting the things they want and in the process, further strengthening their conviction in their limiting belief.

Then there is the belief that the world has just enough to offer to the people in it. This school of thought is interesting as it is slightly more positive than the one before. Despite this, it cannot be said to be the product of a positive mindset. Sadly, the grand majority of people belong to this school of thought. As such, they believe that the world can offer them just enough to get by on a day-to-day basis. This results in the law of attraction delivering them just enough, of course, which serves as proof of their beliefs. The frustrating thing about this belief system is that it keeps people from seeing, let alone fulfilling their true potential. It ensures that happiness, satisfaction, wealth, fulfilling relationships, and the like remain just out of reach. Abundance thus becomes visible but not attainable.

The final school of thought revolves around the belief that the world has more than enough to offer everyone. This line of thought is the product of an optimistic mindset, as well as what you need to manifest abundance and cultivate an abundance mindset. People who belong to this persuasion wholeheartedly believe that the things that they have in the present, that they have had in the past, and that they will have in the future are more than enough. They feel grateful for all that they have and express that gratitude regularly. They remain forgiving of others and themselves, even when they make mistakes. They are able to see opportunities that they would have missed had they been blinded by more limiting worldviews. Most importantly, though, they believe that the universe is there to serve them and deliver the very things that they want to their doorstep. Since they put this kind of energy out there, the universe happily obliges and does exactly what they want.

As you may have gathered, people who believe that the world has more than enough to offer to everyone, are people who are able to put their trust in the universe and themselves. If you want to manifest abundance, this is exactly what you need to do. This is easier said than done because it entails changing your beliefs and mindset. However, it is not impossible to do by any means. All you have to do is focus on developing a growth mindset, which is otherwise known as an abundance mindset. A growth mindset is the kind of mindset where you believe that you can always develop whatever abilities, skills, and capabilities you've. People who have a growth mindset thus believe in self-improvement. They further believe that they can get everything that they want and that the world has to offer through self-improvement. Not only does this put a lot of positive energy out into the universe, attracting the things they want to them, but it also makes them work harder for the things they want, whether they realize it or not.

One of the benefits of having a growth mindset is that it makes you focus on the things you should be focusing on to manifest abundance. It prevents you from wasting energy and time by, say, focusing on things like appearing more intelligent or knowledgeable than you actually are. This, as it happens, is something that people with scarcity or fixed mindsets all too often do. The key reason people who have a growth mindset are able to do all this is that they are able to see, acknowledge, and accept their weaknesses without judging themselves (Christian, 2020). That is not to say that they don't work on these weaknesses. They absolutely do. But they are able to recognize these points and work to refine them. In the process, they can learn new things and grow as individual human beings, creating more opportunities to manifest abundance for themselves in the process.

Simultaneously, people who have growth mindsets are able to recognize and improve upon the strengths that they already have. In doing so, they can get even better at what they do and attract even more abundance into their lives. With all this being the case, the question is how are you supposed to cultivate a growth mindset in the first place? Cultivating a growth mindset begins with identifying the kind of mindset you have (Fran, 2022). The most basic way you can do this is to ask yourself what you think about the world. Do you inherently believe that there is more than enough in the world or that there just is not enough? If your answer was the latter or even that there is just enough for everyone, then sadly you possess a scarcity, that is to say fixed, mindset. Another great way you can go about figuring out your mindset is to objectively look at how you approach a challenge, any challenge, that is presented to you. Is your go-to reaction one of doubt, where you express hesitancy about your ability to meet this challenge or is it one where you express eagerness to meet it? Are you more likely to pass on a challenge because you don't know how to do something or are you more likely to accept it because you believe in your ability to learn and then execute exactly what you need to do?

After identifying your mindset, you can start working on changing it. Start by determining what your general strengths and weaknesses are. Then, focus on improving them. Remember, no one expects you to be perfect at the things that you do and you shouldn't either. Expecting and seeking perfection will not ever help you develop an abundance mindset. Seeking constant improvement will, because it recognizes that you can always do better and always give and receive more (Davis, 2019). The best thing you can do when cultivating a growth mindset is to embrace your weaknesses and imperfections. Only then will you be able to grow from them. A great way to change the way you think about your weaknesses and imperfections is to make a conscious effort to attach the word "yet" to thoughts that are associated with it. Say that you're learning how to code. you are a novice, so when people ask you how you are at coding you keep saying and thinking "I am not very good" or "I don't know a lot." A great way to amend these more negative thoughts might be turning them into "I am not very good at it yet" or "I don't know a lot yet." This way, you can give yourself and the universe the message that you're getting better at coding and learning more with each passing day and will get to where you want to be in time.

Striving to turn negative self-talk linked to your skills and abilities into positive self-talk is incredibly effective in cultivating a growth mindset. This is why writing down any negative statement you might be making about your abilities and then working on them the same way you do with other negative thoughts is a good idea. Another good idea is to make a conscious effort to see challenges, difficulties, and even problems as "opportunities". Replacing such words with the word "opportunity" in your mind accomplishes two things: It makes you consider the issue at hand from new, unexpected angles, helping you to find a solution for it more quickly, and it shifts your perspective about it, helping you to develop a more positive outlook. This puts a more positive energy out into the universe, which in turn attracts the kind of solution that will really make you shine brightly among others.

One last thing you can do to cultivate a growth and abundance mindset is to seek other, trusted people's feedback on how you can improve your weaknesses. A lot of us balk at the idea of receiving feedback because we confuse it for criticism and think that it means we have done something wrong. However, that is not what feedback is about, at least not when you approach it with the right mindset. Like challenges and problems, honest feedback can be an opportunity. It can be an opportunity to see where and how you might improve upon yourself. It can be a tool you can use to see and then start working on your own blind spots. Since receiving feedback can help you to fix your weaknesses and blind spots, it can prevent you from making mistakes, which can help you feel more positive about yourself overall. This will further improve the energy and messages you send out into the universe, making you manifest abundance in, well, abundance.

Effort and Positive Emotional States

If you want to manifest abundance, then you have put in the necessary effort for it. This means putting in the work, but it also means making an effort to develop the right emotional states for abundance. Imagine that you are at work: You have a deadline that is coming up and you're quite stressed as a result. You have a lot on your plate too, so you are feeling pretty overwhelmed too. You keep trying to finish your work but things keep going wrong, upsetting you and slowing down your progress. The computer keeps fritzing out, the printer keeps getting jammed, and there seems to be something wrong with the internet, almost bringing things to a grinding halt. You have probably been in a situation like this and have found yourself wondering why such a thing is happening. The short answer is that it is because you are putting all the wrong energy and messages into the universe getting caught in the wrong emotional states (Davis, n.d.). Yes, you're doing the physical work you are supposed to be doing, but you're making an effort to get into the kind of emotional state that would allow you to work best and send positive, helpful energy into the universe. In other words, you are unconsciously sabotaging your own efforts to do well.

Developing the right, that is to say most positive emotional states you can, is a must to manifest abundance. Positive emotional states draw solutions and ease your way, making you get a lot more done, a lot more quickly. Negative emotional states—ones characterized by things such as anxiety, fear, and frustration—attract nothing but problems. Positive emotional states fall into two categories: High energy ones like joy and excitement, and low energy ones like peace and calm. High energy emotions are great because they can get you motivated to do your work, try new things, and even take healthy risks. Low energy emotional states can help you to work steadily to get things done at a pretty rapid pace. They can prevent you from becoming swept up by negative emotions when you encounter challenges and fuel your ability to persevere.

So how can you get into the right emotional states and thus ensure you're spending the right kind of effort to cultivate a growth mindset and manifest abundance? One example of how you might achieve this to reflect on your strengths. Previously, you saw that it was important to consider your weaknesses as growth opportunities (Mignona, 2021). It is equally as important for you to consider and reflect on your various strengths. Contrary to what you might think, your strengths are not just things you're good at. The things you have the potential to be good at, the things that you enjoy doing and that seem to energize you, and the things that have different benefits for you also count as your strengths.

So, you can identify some of your strengths by asking yourself what things you're good at or enjoy doing or are energized by. You can also ask other people what they think your strengths are, because sometimes your friends and family members have a clearer view of our capabilities than you do yourself. If you're going to ask others about your strength, you should try to talk to about 10 people at least. That way you can see which points everyone agrees on and get a more comprehensive picture of yourself. Speaking of pictures, you can use this information you've obtained to paint a self-portrait of sorts. By bringing together what you think your strengths are and what other people have said, you can develop a thorough understanding of your abilities. You can then focus and double down on them. For instance, you can make a point to use your identified strengths more in your work. Thanks to this you'll both end up in a more positive emotional state, which'll make, say, work a lot easier for you, and do better at work, your social life, and anything else that you tackle. This combination will attract abundance your way in all its different ways and forms.

An additional way of improving and increasing your efforts and manifesting abundance is to try and find the silver lining in tough or challenging situations. You already know that learning to view challenges as opportunities is a great manifestation technique. So is learning to find the silver lining when things look a little bleaker than they usually do (Prilleltensky, 2020). The thing about life is that it is not always made up of rainbows and roses. Instead, life is all about taking the good with the bad and overcoming the hurdles that pop up in your way every once in a while. There is no getting around these hurdles, so fuming at the fact that they are there or feeling defeated in the face of them is not going to help you. If anything, those things will put the wrong messages out into the universe, making it hard, if not impossible for you to overcome them.

Learning to find the silver lining in problematic situations does the exact opposite of this. This is because silver linings remind you of all the things that you still have in your life that you should be grateful for. They thus generate positive feelings that help keep negative thoughts at bay. Furthermore, they enable you to see situations from new, unexpected angles. This makes it possible for you to keep pushing through under tough circumstances and increases both your resilience and your ability to persevere.

Process and Perseverance

It can be said, in that case, that effort and perseverance go hand in hand a bit. Perseverance is a must have ingredient for anyone seeking to manifest abundance. Perseverance is your ability to keep going whenever you're faced with tough or challenging situations and circumstances. It is something that can help you to remain positive and keep negative thoughts and emotions back. Perseverance works best if you know exactly why you want to manifest abundance. This is because your "why" becomes a motivating factor for you, a reminder as to why you're doing everything that you're doing. This "why", when expressed clearly and positively, builds your resilience, strengthens your perseverance, and fuels your manifestation abilities.

An important caveat to note here is that this is only true for those cases where the intentions behind your "why" are true to your values and pure (Michelle, 2023). Let us say that you're trying to manifest abundance because you've been working very hard and would like to go on a nice vacation where you can relax with your friends and spend quality time with them. The intentions behind this "why" are certainly pure as they are all about taking care of yourself and strengthening the bonds you have with your valued friends. Depending on what kind of person you are, these intentions align with your personal values too. What if you were trying to manifest abundance because that is what everyone seems to be doing and you feel like you should? Well, then, your intentions can't really be said to be pure since you don't really seem to believe in them in the first place. They likely don't align with your personal values too, which means you'll not be able to get on the right wavelength to manifest abundance like this (Sasson, 2009).

How can you determine what your "why" is and see whether the intentions behind them are pure or not? You start by writing down what, precisely you're trying to manifest within the context of abundance. Then you ask yourself what it is you hope to get or achieve by manifesting it. Of course, you try to answer that question as honestly as you can. Once you have your answer, or answers as the case may be, you ask whether it aligns with your values? If you are unsure what your values are, one exercise that will help you to determine them is to write your personal mission statement, which you already know how to do from the Manifesting Love chapter. The couples mission statement exercise found in that chapter can very easily be adapted into a solo exercise. As such, it can help you attain real clarity where your values are concerned.

If your "why" does align with your values, then the next question you need to ask yourself is whether it is something you truly want to receive or achieve. The easiest way to determine this is to ask yourself whether you're trying to manifest this because everyone else is or not? If you're doing something just because others are or because they think everyone should, then that probably is not something you crave deep down. That, unfortunately, means that you can spend a lot of time and effort trying to achieve something you don't actually want and end up not getting it. After all, the universe is bound to recognize the fact that you don't want what you're striving for through the energy you're sending out into the world. Hence, it will not be able to deliver your goal to you anymore than you'll be able to manifest it or attract it your way.

Of course, none of this can be said for things that you really want to achieve and that you have pure reasons for wanting to achieve. When these two things come together, they not only put the law of attraction to some real use but they also increase your resilience and perseverance. In doing so, they ensure that you remain motivated and positive through tough situations and thus able to keep manifesting and able to continue putting in all the effort that is required.

Having said all that, perseverance can at times be a difficult trick to master. It comes in handy in tough situations and when facing challenges but such circumstances can get the better of even the most positive among us, from time to time. This is why actively cultivating perseverance at all times, even in positive moments, is so important.

Luckily, there are several techniques you can use to do this, such as hypnosis.

Why Hypnosis Works

The idea of manifesting abundance by using hypnosis might sound a little weird, but the fact that it works is by now undeniable. Hypnosis is a genuine manifestation technique that essentially helps you to attain an altered consciousness which makes manifestation easier to do. Hypnosis has long since been acknowledged as an effective mental technique. This is why it is often used by medical professionals to address a number of health issues. For example, hypnosis is known to prove effective in pain control, including the kind of pain that you experience when you get a burn, when you're giving birth, and when you're undergoing a dental procedure (Mayo Clinic Staff, 2022). Hypnosis is known to help with hot flashes that are the wonderful side effects of menopause. It is even used by oncologists when they are treating different patients with cancer, as it helps deal with the side effects of radiotherapy and chemotherapy.

On top of all this, hypnosis is known to reduce anxiety disorders, like phobias, and help treat behavioral problems. That being the case, it shouldn't be too surprising to find out that hypnosis can be a manifestation tool. Within the context of manifestation, hypnosis is most often used to help you temporarily suspend any limiting beliefs you may have. In the process, it makes you believe with greater force in the very things you're trying to manifest and increases your positive thoughts and feelings (Wong, 2021b). As such, it helps you achieve vibrational alignment between the things that you want and the energy that you're sending out into the universe.

To manifest abundance through hypnosis, you have to first figure out exactly what you want to manifest. For argument's sake, let us say that it is financial abundance you're trying to manifest. Now, you'll have to find a hypnosis online that is targeted to help you manifest it. Fortunately, there'll be a ton of hypnosis videos you can find on YouTube, as well as numerous apps you can try. You may have to try a couple of different videos until you find one that works for you. Once you do, you'll need to sit down or lie down in a comfortable position, so that you can focus on clearing away any negative thoughts, feelings, and energy that might be surrounding you. Your energy is the point of attraction where manifestation is concerned, after all, meaning it has to be positive for you to attract positive things. There are a couple of things you can do to clear your energy before beginning your hypnosis practice. Mindfulness meditation is one example. Another is breathing exercises. Writing in your manifestation journal can be yet another. A manifestation journal is simply a journal where you write down all the various things you want to attract, as you'll recall.

After clearing your energy, you'll need to work entering into a more relaxed state of being. The best way to do this is lie down on your back somewhere comfortable. Make sure the lights are dim before you do and go ahead and light any candles you'd like for ambiance. Obviously, make sure you're wearing something comfortable too. Next, close your eyes and take 10 deep, slow breaths in a row. Inhale through your nose and exhale through your mouth, feeling your diaphragm rise and fall as you go. Keep your eyes closed as you breathe in and out. Focus on relaxing each and every one of your muscles as you breathe and make sure to make note of and work on any points of tension you find. If you're sufficiently relaxed, then you can turn on your hypnosis video at last. As you listen to the video or recording, try to visualize everything that is being described in the video. More specifically, visualize yourself having already achieved everything that is being described. Make your visualizations as vivid, detailed, and realistic as you can.

It is important that you don't berate yourself while doing your hypnosis practice should your mind wander off. Like in meditation, this is perfectly normal and can happen from time to time. When it does, all you need to do is very gently bring your attention back to the practice and refocus. After that, you just need to keep going as you are until the practice comes to an end. Now, it might be that you're hesitant to try a hypnosis practice due to time constraints, especially if you already do something like meditation on a regular basis. One thing you can try in such a case is to put on your hypnosis video right before you go to bed and listen to it while you sleep. You might think that this would not work, but it is actually more effective than you know. This is because your subconscious mind, which is responsible for around 90% of all the decisions you make if you'll remember, will be listening and paying attention to the messages your hypnosis recording will be giving while you sleep. Hence, it will pick up on those messages and start truly believing in them. This will make you adopt a more positive outlook in many ways and enable you to start attracting the kinds of things that you want.

That being said, it typically takes around 40 days for hypnosis practices to turn into regular habits and thus for them to make it possible for you to really manifest abundance. That means that you'll have to be just a little patient where hypnosis is concerned. Actually, you'll have to be a little patient where manifestation, in general, is concerned too. The abundance you manifest is not going to be delivered unto your doorstep in the span of a single day, as was mentioned before. Rather it is going to take some time for you to receive that which you're attracting. It is vital that you keep this fact in mind when you're manifesting. Otherwise, you can get disheartened and give up too soon, which'll be a shame.

The Importance of Patience

They say that patience is a virtue but they often forget to mention that it is the hardest virtue to maintain. This is especially true when you're manifesting abundance, since it means you have to keep on the lookout for the things you're trying to attract. Lose your patience too soon and give up and you'll never get whatever it was you were trying to manifest. Later on, you may even find out that you had been incredibly close to achieving it, if only you'd have been just a little more patient.

Impatience is something you generally want to avoid when you're manifesting something, but especially when you're trying to attract abundance. This is because impatience is too often colored by things like fear and worry, which messes with your vibrational alignment with the universe. The good news is that this is a fixable matter, so long as you take the right approach when dealing with your impatience. Getting made at yourself or chastising yourself for getting impatient, for example, is not going to be of any help to you. If anything, it is going to mess with your alignment even more, making things ever more difficult. Since impatience is a negative emotion, the more negativity you feed into it in the form of admonishments, for example, the worse things will get and of course, your chastisements will not do away with your impatience anyways.

What are you to do, then, when you find yourself getting impatient? In all honesty, the best thing you can do in this case is to forgive yourself for being impatient. We are all human, which means that we all experience more negative emotions and emotional states from time to time. You're not the only individual on planet earth to ever experience impatience. It is important that you remind yourself of this most basic act when you find yourself getting impatient. It is equally as important that you take a deep, calming breath when you feel the impulse to get mad at yourself for this and let it go as you breathe out. It is vital that you tell yourself that you're allowed to err every once in a while and repeat to yourself that you forgive yourself for your impatience. Accepting the forgiveness you're offering yourself may take a little bit of time and effort. That is perfectly alright. But as with things like positive affirmations, repeating your forgiveness regularly to yourself should help. If you want, you can always create positive affirmations that aim to increase your ability to forgive yourself. You can also craft ones that increase your patience and hold impatience at bay, so long as you remember to repeat them every day.

Another thing you can do to become a more patient human being is to try to get used to the idea of relinquishing control and surrendering yourself to the universe. The thing about the law of attraction is that you never know exactly when the universe will deliver that which you're manifesting to you. So, why worry and stress about something that is completely out of your control. One question you can ask yourself to get better at "surrendering" is "Am I doing everything that I should be doing to get what I want?" If the answer to that question is yes, then what you need to do is not to anxiously wait around, but take a deep breath and relax. This may prove difficult to do at first, but you can always remind yourself that by focusing on relaxing, you're putting more positive energy into the universe and strengthening your manifestation abilities in the process.

Practicing relaxation techniques, such as meditation should be of great help to you in this regard. So can working on developing a sense of certainty. A sense of certainty is something that goes hand in hand with the trust you place on the universe and in your own abilities. One way to develop this sense is to ask yourself how you'll feel when you receive the thing you're manifesting. Will you feel more relaxed and calmer? Will you be relieved and really happy? Consider how you'd act once you go through the thing you were manifesting. Now, take out a notebook or pull up a Word document and write all your answers down. Read over them when you're finished and try to embody them whenever you feel your impatience levels spiking up. If you think this sounds very similar to acting-as-if, then you'd be correct.

By working to curb your impatience and improve your patience, you can make the process of manifestation both easier to do and a more relaxing endeavor than you'd think. Thanks to your high patience levels, you'll be able to manifest all sorts of wonderful things, like abundance. Patience, though, can be especially helpful in manifesting one other vital component of life, which is success.

Chapter 5:

Manifesting Success

There is little success where there is little laughter. –Andrew Carnegie

Success is something that everyone wants to achieve in life, no matter their age, nationality, or anything else for that matter. Yet success can often be elusive, not because it is inherently hard to achieve but because everyone's definition of success is different. One person's definition of success might be starting a non-profit that can really help people, for instance. Another's might be achieving a level of wealth that would allow them and their family to live very comfortably. Still another's might be turning their passion into a job, even if it means they will not become a millionaire through it or living a lifestyle where they can surf on the beach every day. Since everyone's definition of success is different, manifesting success necessitates figuring out what your own, personal definition of it is.

Success can only be considered real success if you feel truly fulfilled through it. Say that you work a corporate job and are very high up in the corporate hierarchy. You make really good money and the people around you all consider you to be very successful. The problem is that your job does not fulfill you by any definition of the word. At best, it bores you. At worst, it drains you and just makes you feel unhappy. Can you really consider yourself to be successful then, even if your job has ensured your financial security? No, you cannot (Roy, 2022). True success is not just about financial or material stability or well-being you see. It is equally about your emotional and spiritual well-being. If you find yourself in a position where you're financially well off but spiritually and emotionally bankrupt then you're going to have put in some good hard work figuring out your definition of success. That way, you'll be able to put in the work necessary to start manifesting it in your life.

Figuring out your own, personal definition of success requires creating a vision of success. In other words, it requires deciding what success looks like for you. Overall, three components go into shaping your vision of success. These are your lifestyle, your creative freedom, and your financial stability. In keeping with that, the first question you have to ask yourself is what kind of lifestyle do you want to lead? Your lifestyle includes all sorts of things like your social life, your relationships with your friends, family, and partner, your general health and well-being, the kind of holidays you'd like to be able to take, and what hobbies you have or would like to have. Ask yourself how you'd like your life to look like on all these different fronts. For instance, do you want to be in a big city like New York or would you rather live somewhere more rural, where things are slower and calmer? Would you like to be going from event to event and lead a bustling lifestyle or do you just want to be able to hang out with a valued group of friends regularly. How much time do you currently have to spend on your hobbies? Do you even have any hobbies? Are there any you'd like to do more of or pick up? How do you want to spend your day-to-day life? How many hours do you want to spend in the office? How much free time would you rather have?

Try to write down the answers to all these questions and any other ones you can think of. Try to see the ideal lifestyle you'd like to live in your mind's eye as you do. That done, you can move on to creative freedom, which refers to the things that make work feel meaningful and worthwhile to you. Start by listing the things that you're passionate about and that motivate you. Is there any way you can incorporate these things into your work in any way? What are the projects that you most liked working on in the past? What did you like about them so much? How about your work environment? What does your ideal work environment look like? For example, would you prefer to go to the office or are you more of a work-from-home kind of person? What are your current colleagues like? Do you enjoy working with them? If so, what are the things you enjoy most about them? If not, what kinds of colleagues would you rather work with? How much creative freedom or freedom in general do you have at work? Is that something you're happy with or would having more be ideal for you? Would you rather have a greater sense of freedom outside of work and thus, more free time to pursue your passions?

Give careful thought to your work and work environment by answering questions like these. Try to paint a picture of your ideal work life based off of these answers. That done, move onto financial stability. In considering this, try to define what financial success would have to look like for you to live the kind of lifestyle you've outlined in your notebook. What is the "more-than-enough"—not minimum or "just enough," mind you—figure you'd have to earn in order to be able to live this lifestyle you've envisioned? Try to get as specific as you possibly can in answering this last question as it will make manifesting both success and wealth easier. Try to identify what your personal income goals are as you think about this, but also how you'd need to budget to have your ideal savings, and things like how much you could give to charity. Once you've figured out all these specifics and numbers, take in your answers in all three categories we have covered so far. If you're truly satisfied with them, then pick up your pen and write down exactly what success looks like and means for you.

There are a couple of additional things you need to keep in mind when you're writing this definition down, of course. For one, it is important that your definition be written in a positive way, using positive language (Lowe-MacAuley, 2023). For another, it is equally as important that you're honest with yourself when writing your definition of success. This might be hard to do because society has its own, widely accepted definition of success, one that we are expected to adopt and conform to. If your definition of success does not match it, then you may struggle with it some. Ultimately though, being honest with yourself and accepting what success means to you personally, however different it might be from what it means to others, is the only real recourse. It is the only way you can manifest what you want, lead a fulfilling life, and start manifesting the kind of success you want.

Goal Setting Once More

Getting clear on your definition of success is a great first step to take on your journey to manifest it. It is, however, just that: A first step. Your second step is to figure out what goals you need to set and meet in order to be able to make your vision of success your reality. This is where

SMART goals come to the picture once more. As a quick reminder SMART goals stand for:

Specific

Measurable

Achievable

Realistic

Time-based

It is important that your goals be SMART because that is the only way you can ensure you can actually realize them. As you're deciding on what your goals are, it is equally as important that you write them down. Writing your goals down is an effective visualization strategy because it makes you 76% more likely to achieve them. It makes you better able to recall them by as much as 65% too, which is great if you have a lot of different goals you'd like to meet (Axe, 2020). Writing down your goals has several other benefits on top of that, including helping you to stay motivated, narrowing down your focus so that your actions align better with your goals, and making your progress more measurable, which is doubly motivating. There is also the fact that writing goals down increases your level of productivity. This is because it makes you instantly better at time management. When you know exactly what you need to achieve, you work faster and you get better at prioritization, which is a vital part of achieving success (Pettit, 2020).

If you want to meet your goals and achieve success, then you need to develop a prioritization process and a goal hierarchy. A prioritization process helps you figure out which tasks you need to do first to achieve your goals and a goal hierarchy allows you to prioritize the various goals that you have. Both of these are essential because they enable you to focus your efforts on the most important and essential things you have to do and thus, use your time efficiently. They help you manifest success better by directing your thoughts, focus, and attention where they need to go, thereby drawing success to you in a much quicker fashion. They help you to see which short term goals you need to complete first, in order to achieve your long term goals.

With all that being said, how exactly do you prioritize goals and tasks? You use a handy tool called the Eisenhower Matrix, which was created by President Eisenhower, hence the name. The Eisenhower Matrix divides your tasks and goals into four categories. These are:

- urgent and Important
- urgent but Not Important
- important but Not Urgent
- not Urgent and Not Important

Of these categories, the tasks and goals you need to prioritize first is Urgent and Important. Goals that fit into this category ask that you take immediate action on them or suffer rather extreme consequences. Your next priority after that category is Urgent But Not Important. These are goals and tasks you can delegate. They need to be done for you to achieve the things you want, but unlike the first category they can be taken care of by someone else, instead of you. Meanwhile, Important but Not Urgent goals denote tasks that you can schedule. They will have great benefits for you once completed and take you a step closer to your goals, but they can be done tomorrow, rather than today. As for Urgent and Not Important tasks, these are things that you can simply remove from your to-dos. In other words, you can delete them, which you should do seeing as this'll save you a great deal of time and energy, helping you to focus more on the things you want, thus making the law of attraction work better for you (Scroggs, 2021).

As you may have noticed, it is not just your goals that you can fit into these categories. It is your task as well, which you can think of as the steps you need to take to achieve your various goals. Knowing how to prioritize your tasks can make manifesting success a great deal easier, but first you need to be able to divide your goals into tasks. A great way of achieving this is to start by dividing your long term goals into short term ones. You can then divide those into even shorter, mini goals, if you can (Spearity Team, 2023). Only after that can you determine what tasks you need to complete to be able to meet that mini goal. You can get to work on this by asking yourself what exactly you need to do to achieve the thing you want. As with your goals, you have to be as specific as you can be when writing these tasks down. Remember, manifestation loves specificity! Try to get as detailed as you can in creating your tasks and, again, make sure they are measurable, achievable, realistic, and time-bound. Having written your tasks down, try to start each day by reviewing your tasks. That way you can get into the exact right mindset to send the best, most productive energy out into the universe and keep manifesting even as you work.

Dividing your goals into tasks, prioritization, and even goal setting work best when you make sure that the goals you've chosen align with your dreams, passions, and the vision of success you've crafted with your own two hands. Goals that don't align with these things will prevent you from manifesting success since they will be counter to your definition of it. The same can be said for goals that you're not able to control for yourself. If your ability to meet a certain goal is dependent on someone other than you, then manifesting success will be infinitely harder for you. If, on the other hand, whether you can meet a goal is dependent on your actions, then there is no reason why you can't manifest the success you dream of. The kinds of actions you want to take in order to be able to manifest success are called aligned actions. Aligned actions are the purposeful steps you take—meaning those tasks you consciously complete—to achieve the things you want. Such actions are always in line with your dreams, desires, beliefs, and values, which is why they work (Cardinale, 2023).

Put simply then, taking aligned actions is your way of actively participating in the manifestation process. Otherwise known as inspired actions, these are always positive behaviors and attitudes, which means that they increase the positive energy you're putting out there (Wong, 2021c). It is important to note here that aligned actions require a certain degree of surrender. When you are undertaking an aligned action, you are obviously being active and doing your best to reach your goals. Once you're done, however, you need to surrender to the outcome of that action, whatever it may be. This is something that can make taking aligned action challenging for some, since they believe surrendering is a passive, maybe even negative thing. Surrender is neither passive nor negative though, as it is not about being defeated, giving up, or anything of the sort. Instead, it is about trust. It is about trusting yourself to know that you did all that you could and trusting the universe to bring success you're manifesting to you. In these senses, the act of surrendering is actually a very active kind of behavior, one that increases positive thinking and positive energy.

If surrendering to the outcome of your actions is a challenge for you, then affirmations or even prayer can be of help to you. Writing down positive affirmations or prayers that affirm your trust and belief in both the universe and yourself, then repeating them whenever you feel fear or doubt creep in can help you to embrace surrender. You can turn to these affirmations or prayers whenever you feel your impatience levels rise up too. In this way, you can increase your cooperation with the universe even more. You may even find that they make other manifestation techniques, such as visualization, more powerful and thus more uplifting.

Visualization Techniques for Success

Visualizing success becomes a whole lot easier to do once you determine what success looks like for you. Visualization is an essential technique for manifesting success and a proven one at that too. Studies have found that people who visualize success become more confident in their ability to achieve it, for example. To be specific, it has been found that such people are typically 67% more confident in this regard than others (Axe,

2020). Generally speaking, visualization seems to be especially good for manifesting success. That is why there are many different visualization techniques that have been developed specifically for manifesting success, starting with mental rehearsals.

A mental rehearsal is a psychological visualization technique that has you envision yourself performing a certain activity. Mental rehearsal is an exercise that actors use a lot before they are to go on stage. If you were an athlete, for instance, then you might mentally rehearse a game you're about to play. If you were about to go in for a big job interview, then you might mentally rehearse how it will go and how you'll answer the questions you're being asked (Sabater, 2022).

One of the great benefits of mental rehearsal is that it can soothe and tamp down any negative feelings you may have like anxiety, stress, and worry, about whatever it is you're about to do. In the process it helps you to relax a little and fosters more positive feelings for your undertaking. This, in turn, makes you more productive, creative, and removes any limiting beliefs and mental blocks that might be standing in your way. Mental rehearsal is so effective that it affects you on a neurological level. According to one study, when you engage in mental rehearsal the neurons in your brain associated with the actions you'll be performing start firing up. Say that you're mentally rehearsing a basketball game and are picturing yourself shooting a three-pointer. In this case, the neurons in charge of dictating the actions of the various muscles responsible for directing the actions of your muscles would start firing up. They would do so despite the fact that you're not physically performing those actions at that particular moment (Natraj & Ganguly, 2018).

Mental rehearsal is a very specific form of process visualization, as you might have gathered. It proves most effective when you do it right before you have to physically perform the task you're imagining. Like with all other visualization techniques, it gets to be even more effective when you make your imagination as detailed and vivid as you possibly can. It is typically recommended that you find somewhere calm before you start your practice. This way you'll be able to improve your focus and approach the practice with a calmer frame of mind. Start your mental rehearsal by simply sitting down somewhere comfortable and slowly taking deep breaths (Sabater, 2022). Try to calm down as much as possible, especially if you're experiencing some nerves. Once your heart rate has settled down a bit, you can start visualizing what it is you're going to do. The trick here is to imagine yourself actually performing the required actions, as opposed to watching from the outside. You're not an audience member sitting in the theater watching the performance, after all. You're the main star putting on the show.

As you're visualizing, make sure to imagine every step of the process, no matter how small or seemingly inconsequential. You're not going to be able to skip them in real life, so including them in your rehearsal will only make the practice more realistic. As you picture yourself performing these actions, try to see how calm, collected, and confident you are. Try to see those sentiments reflected in the very actions you're performing. Be sure to envision any challenges you might face and how you'll calmly and successfully overcome them. This way, you'll be able to manifest that calm and success should you face those challenges in real life. You'll also be more prepared for them. Ideally, you want to repeat your mental rehearsal process seven times. This way, it will really stick and you'll send a lot of positive energy into the universe. Don't berate yourself if you're only able to do this six times, as opposed to seven due to time constraints or something like that. That would have the opposite effect of what you're trying to achieve.

Another visualization technique you can try to manifest success is the happy place. As you have, maintaining your calm and remaining confident are essential when you're working toward success. As such, you want to get into the kind of frame of mind that supports such feelings and invites them into your life. This can be hard to do in the moment leading up to major events like a public appearance where you have to give a speech or an interview you have to partake in. Such events will directly impact your success, after all. The happy place visualization is a great tool to use in moments where you experience the sudden onset of nerves and stage fright. It can soothe away the stress you're feeling significantly and boost your confidence levels (Benson et al., 2011).

The happy place visualization requires imagining yourself in your happy place. First though, you must figure out where yours is, as everyone's is rather different. One person's happy place might be their childhood home while another's might be the seaside. Close your eyes and consider where you feel the most peaceful and happiest. Once you have your answer, try to envision yourself in that place in as detailed a manner as you can (Pavlik, 2021). Focus especially on the things that make you feel good in this place. What does the space around you feel like? What does it smell like? How much light is in this place and where, exactly, are you standing in it? Try to use all of your senses as you are imagining your happy place to make it as realistic as you can. If you can't come up with a specific place that makes you happy, you can just choose an environment you'd like to be in. You can go with a sunny beach or a snowcapped mountain top, for example. You can envision a flower-filled meadow or rolling fields. As you're picturing these places, feel free to let your imagination run wild. If you're still having trouble envisioning a good happy place for yourself or staying focused on it, one thing you can try is a happy place meditation. There are plenty of such meditations you can find on YouTube and many more on the various meditation apps out there. Simply pull up a guided one and follow along to the directions they provide you with. Actually, a happy place meditation is not the only kind of meditation you can take up to manifest success. There are many others to choose from, all of which can be helpful to you in a variety of ways.

Meditation for Success

By now, your manifestation toolkit is likely brimming with tools and techniques, each of which is more effective than the last. Of these, meditation is one of the most effective and versatile ones. It is also one that the great success stories of our time swear by. Take the famous entrepreneur Tim Ferris, for instance (Ferriss, 2007). Ferris, who wrote the book *The Four Hour Work Week*, describes meditation as the key to success. To write his book, he interviewed many different CEOs and successful entrepreneurs to discover what their daily, success-manifesting habits were. He quickly found out that meditation was one habit nearly all of them had in common. When he was interviewing Tony Robbins, for example, Robbins declared that meditation was "an hour of power" and stated that developing a meditation habit changed his life. When Ferris interviewed Arnold Schwartzeneger, he learned that he had gotten into meditation back in the 80s. Steven Jobs claimed that meditation was partly responsible for his ability to turn his business into success stories.

Looking at Ferris' book, it is surprising just how many people are willing to sing meditation's praises when it comes to manifesting success. It becomes much less surprising, though, when you consider what kinds of benefits meditation has to offer you. One common characteristic among all the successful people that Ferris' book covers is that they are able to learn, process, recall, and use new information at a frightening pace. These are skills that meditation actively strengthens and develops. Studies show that meditation stimulates the regions of your brain that are responsible for these abilities you see. Not only that, but they actually increase the volume of the gray matter in those same regions of your brain. One study has even found that meditation for just four times a week improved their working memory in just two weeks' time (Patel, 2018).

One of the greatest benefits of meditation is that it eliminates negative thought loops from your mind, which are significant roadblocks when trying to manifest, as you know. Mantra meditation can be especially good for this. Mantra meditation entails repeating a positive phrase that you choose as your mantra.. This brings your conscious attention to that positive thought, making you send more positive energy to the world, rather than on the negative thoughts that keep trying to run through your mind. As with other types of meditation, your mind might sometimes wander off as you. Should that happen, you should gently guide it back to your meditation and the mantra you've been repeating. You should do so without criticizing, judging, or otherwise berating yourself as this will simply distract you and generate a more negative mindset, which is the opposite of what you want.

A positive mindset and positive emotions are crucial for manifesting success and meditation—be it mantra meditation or something else—can help with both. Meditation is a very effective way to process and accept all that you're feeling, including negative emotions. Developing a positive mindset does not mean ignoring or repressing such emotions, you see. Rather, it means understanding what these emotions are trying to tell you, acknowledging and learning from them, and then letting them go. Say that you're feeling angry. Ignoring your anger will not make it go away. If anything, it will color your outlook and behavior and thus have some very poor consequences on your relationships and your work. Looking at your anger objectively, on the other hand, will help you to see the root cause behind it. If that root cause is that someone has crossed a boundary that you set, then you'll know you need to communicate that issue to that person. In doing so, you'll be able to resolve the matter and let go of your anger, keeping it from impacting your energy and sending the wrong messages to the universe in the process.

Meditation is known for its ability to help you to understand your emotions, where they are coming from, and control them (Brazier, 2016). It is further known for calming down especially powerful negative emotions, thus stopping them from coloring your behavior and impacting your relationships with other people. Meditation, then, is a great way of strengthening your relationships. This is important for manifesting success both because your personal definition of success may pertain to your social life and because networking is often a major part of achieving success.

A final benefit that meditation has to offer you is that it can increase your creativity. This is something to keep in mind seeing as creativity, open mindedness, and out-of-the-box thinking are qualities you need to develop to be successful (Patel, 2018). One specific kind of meditation you can try to develop these skills is open-monitoring. Open-monitoring is a kind of meditation where you observe and notice all the phenomena that is taking place around and within you in that particular moment (Delehanty, 2017). This requires keeping your attention and focus rather flexible. Moreover, it urges you to accept all the thoughts, emotions, and sensations that flit in and out of your body without criticizing or judging yourself for them. This might be a little difficult at first, requiring you to remind yourself to abstain from judgment. However, the more you do it, the easier it will become, until one day you notice that you've achieved total awareness of everything you're experiencing without being distracted by them. It is this very benefit that allows you to get more creative, as well as become more focused and even overcome any mental biases you may hold (Voss, 2017). Actually, open-monitoring can be a good way of learning to let go of any negative thoughts and feelings you may have regarding any mistakes you make or any failures you experience. No one likes mistakes and failures, of course, but it is vital that you develop your ability to learn from them, as well as accept them without letting them trap you in a negative mindset, assuming you still want to manifest success.

Failure and Mistakes

Over the years, many of us have come to consider success as this perfect journey. The idea is that success is the kind of journey that only has an upward trajectory. This idea, however, is a fantasy. The road to success is often filled with challenges and obstacles that you must overcome. Sometimes those obstacles prove a little too high or difficult to get over, though. Other times, you simply don't know what method you need to use to overcome them or else you end up making a mistake that prevents you from leaping over them. The thing that most people forget about success is that this is normal. Experiencing failure and making mistakes are part of the journey to achieve success. They are part of your journey to manifest it too, since they are invaluable opportunities for learning and growth. Experiencing these things, then, is not a reason to give up nor do they mean that you'll not be able to manifest success. It just means you'll have to use what you can obtain from them to devise new ways of approaching the obstacle before you.

The problem with failure and mistakes is that they generate a lot of negative feelings that keep sweeping you away and keep you from both learning from them and manifesting success in the process. Such feelings can even cause you to give up on trying again, which is why it is essential that you work on changing your outlook on them. The most obvious way of doing this is learning to look for lessons in failures and mistakes (Hurst, 2016a). Mistakes and failures often happen for a reason. So, why did this particular one happen? What could you do differently in the future so that you don't get the same result as before? What skills can you develop to overcome the obstacle standing in your way? What alternatives can you try in the face of the challenge before you and can you approach the matter at hand from different angles?

Considering questions like this and analyzing the failure you've experienced or the mistake you've made can develop your problem solving and out-of-the-box thinking skills. It can make it possible for you to find new solutions and approaches to tackle problems with. Furthermore, it can make you gain valuable insight and information from the experience you're having, which you'll be able to put to good use going forward. Gaining these insights and information can generate more positive emotions too, thereby fueling your manifestation efforts, rather than becoming a hindrance to them.

A second way you can change your perspective of failure and mistakes is to make an effort to find the silver lining of the situation you are in. This might be a little difficult to do and it might require some creativity on your part, depending on what kind of situation you're faced with.

However, making an effort to do so can help you to change your perspective of the failure or mistake at hand. It can enable you to change your manner of thinking. Say that you had been interviewing for a job you really wanted but ultimately you did not get it. One good side to this seemingly negative development might be that you can find and get an even better job, where you'll be much happier. Another might be that you've avoided rushing into a position, without truly considering your strengths and wants. Alternatively, say that you've just gone through a break up. That is admittedly rough and you're now dealing with all sorts of feelings. The good side to this situation might be that that break up was the right decision to make for your long term happiness. Another might be that you now have a better sense of what you want in a relationship and partner or that you now have the opportunity to reconnect more with yourself.

Forgetting about how important connecting or reconnecting with yourself is all too easy, when you think about it. Often, we get so wrapped up in our day-to-day goings on that we forget to check in with ourselves. Interestingly enough, our mistakes and failures can give us the opportunity to do so. They force us to pause and take a look at what we could have done differently. Many times the answer to that question ends up being "I could have taken things more slowly, without rushing or stressing as much," which would have prevented that mistake or failure. One way to change your perspective of failures and mistakes, then, is to try and see them as opportunities for rest and self-care. This requires being kind to yourself when you experience failure or make a mistake, of course. Self-care is a great way to deal with these things and keep yourself in a positive mindset. For self-care to be effective, however, you have to first allow yourself to feel whatever emotion you're experiencing, even if it is a negative one like sadness. As before, ignoring these feelings will not make them go away. Acknowledging them, however, will take some of their power away and make it easier for us to let them go (Tay, 2021).

The first step to doing this is identifying and labeling whatever emotion you're feeling. Labeling your emotions is important because it helps you to regulate them. That means it keeps you from becoming swept away by your emotions and choosing the direction of your thoughts with greater control instead (Aldao, 2014). Take fear, for example. Fear is a very powerful emotion, one that is difficult to tamp down when it takes hold of you or so we think. It becomes much easier to get a grip on your fear, though, if you actually name it. According to one study, naming your phobias when confronted by their force goes a long way to lessening how much they affect you. This matters in the context of failure and mistakes because of the negative emotions that they cause you to feel. By naming these emotions, you can directly influence how and to what degree they affect you. You can prevent them from altering your perspective and thus seeing failure and mistakes as learning opportunities. Simultaneously, you can make sure they don't keep you from seeing the positive sides of the situation or practice self-care to uplift your spirits. Thus, you can take a much needed break after experiencing, say, failure, recuperate to some degree, and then try again once you're feeling energetic enough. In the process, you can keep manifesting success despite the setback you've experienced. Who knows, perhaps the valuable insights you've gained from your experience will even speed up the manifestation process in the long run. They certainly could impact your internal motivation as well, making you work even harder toward your goals.

Internal vs. External Motivation

The importance of motivation cannot be understated when talking about manifesting success. Motivation is connected to manifestation in two ways. First, it directly impacts the work you put into taking aligned action and working toward your goals. The less motivated you feel to take an action, the more negative energy you'll put out into the world. Thus, you'll be less likely to follow through with that action. Second, it impacts whether you are able to practice manifestation in the first place. Certain kinds of mindsets directly impact how motivated you feel to manifest. Without the proper motivation, you'll not be able to focus on what you need to do. Pretty soon, your manifestation efforts will begin to slide, since you'll be thinking "What is the point?"

The first issue at hand—whether you're motivated enough to put in the work required or not—has to do with your intrinsic motivation. There are two types of motivation, you see: Intrinsic and external. Intrinsic motivation is motivation that comes from within you. External motivation, on the other hand, is motivation that comes from outside sources. Doing something because you're passionate about it and you like doing it, for instance, is an example of intrinsic motivation. Doing something because you keep receiving praise for it is an example of external motivation (Perry, 2022). As a general rule, you want to have high levels of intrinsic motivation, that is if you want to be able to complete the various things you need to do to meet your goals and achieve the success you want. This is because you have the ability to generate a near infinite supply of intrinsic motivation, whereas external motivation is finite and can only get you so far. That is not to say you don't need any external motivation. It can certainly be very helpful to receive praise or encouragement from the people around you. But for the most part, you don't want to rely on solely external motivation. If you do, you'll eventually find it very hard to keep going and remain optimistic in the face of the challenges that appear before you.

Being able to increase your intrinsic motivation has a lot of benefits. People who are able to intrinsically motivate themselves, for example, are able to stay focused on and engaged in their work for longer periods of time. They get a lot of personal satisfaction from their work, which is something that can keep you going under the most stressful of circumstances. Of note, there is how intrinsic motivation is better for your mental health and well-being, especially in the long term, and your sense of self-esteem and confidence. To reap these benefits, you have to work on increasing your intrinsic motivation and that starts with satisfying your most basic psychological needs. These needs are autonomy, relatedness, and competence (Sutton, 2021).

Your first psychological need, autonomy, is the freedom to choose. You have to believe that you have freedom of choice in your actions and decisions in order to have autonomy. Your second psychological need, relatedness, is your ability to identify and deepen how you feel about the things that you do. Relatedness essentially means forming a strong connection to your work, as well as to others. Your final need; competence, refers to you having the skills you need for the path you've chosen for yourself, as well as the opportunity to use and show them off.

So, one way to increase your intrinsic motivation is to ensure that all three of these needs of yours are being met. If they are not being met accordingly, then perhaps you can take a closer look at your work. Is there any way you can become more autonomous at work, for example? Can you work on developing any skills that will increase your sense of competence? How might you come to feel more connected to your goals and aspirations? Try answering these questions in writing and working those answers into your day-to-day work. You would be surprised as to just how big a difference even the smallest of changes can make in increasing your intrinsic motivation.

As a rule, the more passionate you are about something, the more intrinsically motivated you'll be to do it. After all, doing that very thing will give you a sense of enjoyment and accomplishment. That being the case, another way to increase your motivation might be to ask yourself what your passions are (DuBois-Maahs, 2019). Try listing the things that you're passionate about and then try to ascertain whether or not you can make them into a bigger part of your life. Consider your definition of success in concert with your passions. Do the two overlap in any way? If so, how might you leverage that connection to make you even more motivated to keep going? If not, is there any way you can make your passions a greater part of your work and success story?

Take your time answering this latter question, as that answer might not always be so obvious. You may have to put your thinking cap on a little bit and explore different possibilities and avenues of thought. That is perfectly alright. A little creativity can only ever help, not hurt your motivation levels. On the flip side, you can take a closer look at your work and ask yourself what you're most passionate about it. Is it the fact that you're making a big impact in other people's lives through your work? Is it how much freedom of movement and creativity it allows for? Is it how social a lifestyle it pushes you to adopt or something else entirely? Again, write down the things you're passionate about in your work. Then try to explore how you might leverage those passions even more.

Another surefire way to improve your intrinsic motivation is to seek to make an impact on others. Making a positive impact on the people around you or the environment you live in can generate a lot of positive feelings in you. These feelings can then be strengthened by the positive emotions people will display toward you, such as gratitude. All this will result in you finding yourself in a sphere of altruism, so to speak, which will both make you more motivated to keep working and send a lot of positive energy pulsing into the universe. This way, manifesting the success you want will become pretty much reflexive for you.

Moving onto how your intrinsic motivation levels can impact your will to keep manifesting success… A lot of mental work goes into the act of manifesting, as you have, and there are a variety of limiting beliefs that can get in the way of this work. These beliefs can either distract you from what you're trying to do, evoking negative thoughts and feelings in you, and sending negative energy out into the universe in the process, or they can keep you from trying to manifest in the first place. Believing that you're not deserving of the success that you're trying to manifest, for example, will certainly result in the latter. This kind of limiting belief can keep you from putting in the effort required to achieve something, because what would be the point?

If you want to increase your motivation and start manifesting success, then you have to convince yourself that you're deserving of it. Positive self-talk exercise can be wonderful for this, as can positive self-affirmations, so long as you use them regularly, meaning every day. These same practices can help with another significant mental block: Fear of failure. Failure is never a nice feeling, as we have already established. Given that, a great many of us are afraid of failure, as if failing means something major about our character and abilities. It does not. Failure is simply a part of your journey to success, one that you have change your perspective on and get comfortable with. If you don't, then you'll allow this fear to block all your manifestation efforts.

Fear of failure usually stems from worrying about what other people will think about you (Kyle, 2022)."What if people judge me?" is one example of such an underlying worry. Another is "What if I make a fool of myself?" Worrying about being made fun of can be a major mental block, after all, to the point that you might end up replaying this possibility in your mind over and over again. The best way to beat your fear of failure is through finding internal validation. This is because worrying about what other people think of you is something that people who mostly rely on external motivation do. When they lose external validation by doing something that is embarrassing or that they are ashamed of, like experiencing a failure or making a mistake in front of others, their sense of motivation takes a major hit. Unable to pick it back up, they get swept away by negative thoughts and feelings, thus becoming unable to keep manifesting.

People who have a strong sense of internal validation—or self-validation as it is otherwise known, however, don't experience this. Such people are not dependent on other people's regard for their sense of self-esteem, confidence, and motivation, after all. Instead, they are able to find value in themselves and the things that they are doing. They are able to recognize that their work is important because they like doing it and are passionate about it. Most importantly, they are able to accept their mistakes and failures, without their motivation and confidence levels taking a huge hit (Durmonski, 2022). In a word, they are more resilient than externally motivated people. Their ability to feel good about themselves is solely dependent on them and not on others. Such people are usually driven by a desire to create. They welcome constructive feedback from others and are able to use it to better themselves in pursuit of success. Interestingly enough, they're not put off my rejection either. In fact, rejection usually ends up motivating them to work harder and do better in the future so that they can get the things they want. The same goes for any failure they experience and mistakes they make.

Finding internal validation begins with asking yourself a question, as always. That question is "What do I really want?" We often think we know why we do the things that we do. Often, we are wrong. Most of our decisions are governed by our subconscious minds, as you'll recall, and we are not immediately privy to the logic that our subconscious minds follow. If you want to find internal validation, then you must make an effort to understand that logic. Hence, we must question what we want and why we want it. Finding your very own definition of success should help with this but you can always probe that definition a little deeper. Why is it that you're seeking to attain this success? What does it mean for you? What psychological or emotional needs do you think achieving this success will fulfill? How will becoming successful make you feel and what can that feeling be traced back to? By exploring the success you're seeking in a more in depth manner like this, you can gain a clearer understanding of why you're doing the things you do. In the process, you can start taking greater responsibility for your actions, which will further increase your sense of validation.

Taking responsibility for your actions is a form of taking control of your life and acknowledging the control that you already have. It is something that can make you feel more grounded and it can help you to see that any accomplishments you achieve are your doing and yours alone. This can be a very powerful feeling. It can motivate you greatly and drive you to work even harder. It is not just your actions you can take responsibility for, though. It is your emotions as well. A lot of people have the tendency to put the responsibility for their feelings on other people's shoulders. "You made me so angry," they say or "You made me so upset." The thing is, no one can "make" you feel anything. You alone have the power to control and regulate your emotions, no one else. This is something you want to acknowledge if you want to increase your sense of self-validation and motivation, while improving the positive mindset you need to manifest success. By taking responsibility for your emotions, even and especially the negative ones, you can stop them from taking control of you and halting your manifestation efforts.

Taking responsibility for your emotions brings us back to the importance of labeling your emotions, at least as a first step. Your second step, after you've acknowledged the emotion you're feeling, is to acknowledge its source. Start by asking yourself what you're feeling, name it, and then acknowledge that it is there. Acknowledge why you're feeling in this way too. If you're feeling angry, for example, admit the reason why. Do the same when you're feeling upset, sad, or any other kind of emotion. After that, take a look at your behavior so far. If your emotions have been affecting your behavior negatively, then admit to that fact and offer apologies where necessary. This might be difficult to do, especially if you're unused to it, but it will help you feel better in the long run, increase your self-validation and motivation capabilities, and even improve your relationships with others. At the same time, it will make coping with difficult feelings like anxiety, fear, and anger much easier to do, thereby keeping you from getting stuck in any limiting beliefs you may have or negative thought loops.

As you can see, manifesting success is greatly dependent on how you define and see success and feel about yourself. By working on these two things, then, you can manifest your version of success, whatever that might mean. Some people's definition of success can be rather unusual and unexpected. That is perfectly alright and something to be celebrated. Other people's definition might be more traditional, in that it is more focused on monetary gain. That is perfectly alright to, especially since money is the thing that makes the world go round. If money is part of your definition of success, then learning how to manifest it specifically, on top of manifesting success, is important. How does manifesting money differ from manifesting success though and what, specifically, can you do for it? Let us find out.

Chapter 6:

Manifesting Money

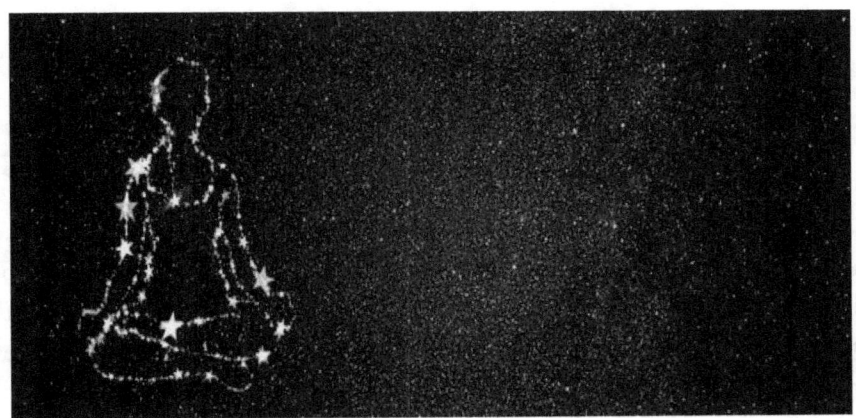

Money is usually attracted, not pursued.—Jim Rohn

Manifesting money is a little different than manifesting wealth, in that it is something that can be done in the short and long term, whereas manifesting wealth is a more long-term process. Manifesting money can be considered a part of manifesting wealth, but it is also something that you can focus on specifically. Likewise, it can be considered a part of manifesting abundance and manifesting success, again depending on what your personal definition of success is.

A lot of people hold onto certain limiting beliefs regarding money, wealth, and abundance, as you'll remember from the previous chapters. Manifesting money requires letting go of these beliefs, which further requires acknowledging the source that they come from. Your personal beliefs about money shape your relationship with it and these beliefs typically arise from your past experiences. To manifest money, you must first acknowledge—not ignore or deny—these past experiences—and focus on healing any money-related trauma you may have experienced. Otherwise, you'll be helpless to stop your stress responses from kicking in any time anything money-related pops up. These stress responses will become significant money blocks, preventing all attempts at manifestation.

Acknowledging Your Past

The experiences you've had in the past define the way you interpret and see things in your present and thus, affect how your future will be shaped. This is just as true for your relationship with money as it is with anything else. Say that you have experienced money-related trauma when you were young. Left unacknowledged and unprocessed, that trauma will leave deep imprints on how you view and deal with money. As a result, your trauma will be triggered anytime you have to deal with having to spend money (Moussu, 2021). It will not matter whether you're spending money for basic necessities, like paying your bills and doing grocery shopping, or having dinner with friends once in a while. No matter the reason, your stress response will immediately kick into gear, making adrenaline and cortisol—the stress hormone—flood your system. This will make your heart start pumping really fast and increase the rate of your breathing. While that is going on, your mind will go into overdrive, riddled with negative thoughts where you're worrying about your finances, ability to save, and worst case scenarios. These will only help increase your stress levels, making your heart pump even more blood to your arms and legs.

This is the typical stress-response your body gives when it encounters a "threat". The idea is that by pumping more blood to your extremities, your body will energize them so that you can either run away really quickly or fight whatever threat that is coming your way. The problem with this, of course, is that trauma related to money is not exactly a physical threat. Hence, it is neither something you can actively run away from nor fight off. It is important that you get this fight or flight response under control when it is triggered by money-related issues for several reasons. For one, not getting it under control will cause you to send a lot of negative energy to the universe, thus blocking your ability to manifest money. For another, the stress you feel will make it all but impossible for you to think logically and rationally. This will make it hard for you to find effective solutions when facing financial difficulties and spot opportunities to generate more money.

There are two things you can do to calm down your fight-or-flight response when it is triggered by money-related issues. One of these is a short term method that can help you calm yourself in that given moment. The other is a long-term method that can help you to process the trauma that is being triggered, thereby ensuring that such a thing will not happen again. The short term method you can use to settle your fight-or-flight response is deep breathing. Deep breathing is a method of voluntarily and consciously slowing down your breathing, helping you to slide into a calmer frame of mind. To practice deep breathing, you should sit down in a comfortable, if possible quiet place when you feel your stress levels spiking. Keep your back straight and your feet planted firmly on the ground. Then, place one of your hands on your stomach and the other on your ribcage (Purse, 2022). This way, you'll be able to physically feel your breaths as you inhale and exhale. Inhale slowly and deeply, making sure that your belly fills up with breath and expands as you do so. Once your belly, that is to say your diaphragm, is filled with air, let the air move up into your rib cage and upper chest. Slowly exhale through your mouth, making sure to contract your abdominal muscles as you go. Keep going like that for at least a minute, longer if you need to, until you've noticeably calmed down.

The great thing about the deep breathing exercise is that it can be used at any time and in any place. You can turn to it anytime you feel your anxiety levels ratcheting up. Thus, you can keep a major money block from thwarting your manifestation process. This, however, is only a short term technique, as was said before. A more long-term and therefore permanent solution is to uncover the root cause of your money trauma and process it properly. This process begins with identifying what your financial triggers are. Are there any specific situations that cause your worries and anxieties to spike more than others? There probably are and it is important that you identify these so that you can develop strategies for managing them. This can entail deep breathing exercises to remain calm through them, as well as relying on budgeting, which you already know how to do.

Meanwhile, you'll have to focus on healing your financial trauma. You can always seek some outside help with this, of course, but there are things you can do on an individual level too. Writing down your money story, for example, can be very helpful. Writing your money story is a great way of objectively seeing what your relationship with money is like, how your past is affecting it, how you make your financial decisions, and what your personal beliefs and narratives about money are (Geannette, 2021). Your money story starts forming around when you're just a child. You don't necessarily have to have gone through significant financial hardship to have the kind of money story that would impact these things negatively. The things you overhear about money as you grow up, the feelings you pick up on, and how your parents or caregivers talk to you about money all play a part in this.

Removing money blocks and being able to manifest it, then, requires understanding how your personal money story has developed. Only then can you get to work changing it. To figure out what your money story is, you need to start writing down memories from your childhood pertaining to money and finances. You can write both good and bad memories as both will influence your personal story. Once you have gotten all your memories down, you can make note of all the different things you tell yourself about money today. Statements like "I am not good with money," or "I am not generous enough," or "It is selfish to buy things for myself," all count as examples you can list, assuming they are true for you. Next, you'll need to consider both the memories you've written down and the beliefs you currently hold side by side. As you consider these two things, ask yourself

- Was money ever discussed in my home when I was growing up?
- What did my parents/family teach me about money?
- What did they not teach me about money?
- How did I feel when I spent money? What did I think as I spent it?
- How did I feel whenever my family spent money around me?
- How did I feel whenever my family spent money on me?
- How did my parents/caregivers talk about money?
- What were my parents'/caregivers' attitude and demeanor like when discussing money, finances, and similar matters?
- Did I have less or more money than my peers? How did this affect my relationship and interactions with them?

These are just some examples of things you can ask yourself to really formulate your money story. You can come up with more, depending what memories you've put down and what your current beliefs are. By answering these questions, you can give your money story a real solid shape and even identify the things that are triggering for you in it. Having done that, you can also take the steps that are necessary to change your story. The first step you need to take in this regard is to learn to forgive yourself for any past financial mistakes. If you don't, not only will you not be able to change your story, but you'll also find that you become riddled with doubt whenever you have to make a new financial decision. Thoughts like "What if I make a mistake again?" will riddle your mind and guess what the law of attraction will draw your way as a result. That is right, another financial mistake.

Since you want to avoid that one of the best things you can do to start manifesting money is to work on self-forgiveness (Hogan, 2021). Positive affirmations and positive self-talk expressing how deserving you are of forgiveness can be great for this. So can thinking about how you'd react to a friend if they made the same mistake and choosing to talk to yourself the way you'd talk to them. Thinking back on the past mistake, asking yourself what you've learned from it, and what you can do differently in the future should also help.

Your next step is to educate yourself a little bit (Geannette, 2021). After all, a great way to make sure you don't make any financial mistakes going forward and approach money matters with a more careful eye is to learn more about it. This will make you feel a lot more confident when you're managing and spending your money. It will help you to make smart decisions with your earnings, dismantling a lot of money-related anxiety you might be feeling. There are many different things you can learn, where your finances are concerned. From budgeting to investing and to setting financial goals, there are a lot of things to consider. So, the more you learn about these things, the more competent you'll feel and the more positive energy you'll put out into the world, even when you're splurging on one thing or another.

Setting Financial Intentions

Manifesting is largely about intentions, as you know. So, you have to set the right intentions behind your financial decisions. There is a great visualization technique you can use to make sure you do just that. This practice is called "anchoring your intentions" (Baum, 2023). "Anchoring your intentions" is a practice that has you use a physical item, like a piece of jewelry or a favored bottle of perfume, to base or anchor your money manifesting intentions on. Your chosen item here is very important. The good news is that it does not have to be anything expensive or luxurious in any way. It simply has to be something that makes you feel wealthy. If you've a necklace, for example, with faux stones that you got from a random bazaar but that you love wearing because it makes you feel like a million bucks, then that is a good anchor to use.

To anchor your intentions for manifesting money, all you have to do is choose the right, ideally small, therefore easy-to-carry-around item. That way, you can immediately pull it out, look and hold onto it anytime you're trying to manifest. Given the way your chosen item makes you feel, it will serve as a steady reminder of what you're manifesting. Your intentions to manifest will come to mind anytime you catch sight of that item, speeding up the process of manifestation and increasing the power of the law of attraction in the process. A lot of people like using jewelry, particularly ones that are made with crystals that are meant to attract money, abundance, and success. These crystals attract these things because they are known to be at a similar vibrational frequency to the very things you're trying to manifest. Thus, they serve doubly well as anchors. Of course, if crystals are not your thing, you don't have to choose anything with them. As before, all you need to do is choose something that makes you feel good and reminds you of wealth, luxury, money, and the like.

All this is well and good, but what exactly are "intentions" in the first place? Your intentions can be considered another word that is used in place of goals. Your financial intentions are your financial goals, then, and it is vital that you set some for yourself. Aside from being a solid way to manifest money, setting financial goals is a very smart financial strategy. This is because, as with all goals, financial intentions help you to focus your thoughts on what you need to do to achieve the things you want. Put a simple way, financial intentions allow you to lead your life actively and, well, with intention. Without them, the way you live your life becomes far more reactive, which means you have much less control over the consequences of your actions.

The best, that is to say, most effective financial intentions are ones that are SMART and that align with your values. To make sure that your financial intentions align with your values, you have to first get clear on what they are (Sharkey, 2023). Let us say that being family oriented is an important value for you. If that is the case, then you're going to want to spend more time with your family. Spending more time with your family, though, will not be possible if you don't factor in your financial situation, at least to some degree. Going out with your kids—assuming you have any—and your partner will cost some money, after all, and things can get pricey, depending on what you're getting up to. One sound financial intention to set that would align with family orientation as a value would be attaining financial stability. That is a rather vague goal, of course, and will need to be made more specific but as a general intention, it falls in line with the value in question.

When you start setting good financial intentions for yourself, then what you need to do is give careful consideration to your values and write them down. Luckily, you already know the exercises you can use to determine your core values from previous chapters. Once you've established what your most important values are you can get to work on your short and long term financial goals. Again, since you discovered the art of setting goals earlier on, this should be a cinch for you. After writing down all your financial goals, you can get to work ordering and prioritizing them (*How to Set Financial Goals*, n.d.). You can divide larger goals into smaller steps and tasks and use the Eisenhower Matrix to determine their order of importance and urgency. Based on these, you can create a financial timeline for yourself, replete with information about how much you've already saved and how much you've managed to save up.

Having determined your official financial goals and to-dos, you'll want to make sure that all your most basic needs are covered. You'll not be able to meet your goals without meeting these needs first. This includes doing things like saving some money and paying off any debts you may have. If you have done that, you can get to the larger task of linking your financial goals with your values and intentions. Making sure that your goals are aligned with your core, personal values is a sure way of increasing your motivation to meet them.

Finally, you'll want to create a financial plan that works for you, which, for the record, would count as taking aligned action to manifest money. The steps for creating a financial plan are pretty simple. You'll already have done the first one by setting financial goals. Your second step will be to keep careful track of your money. That way, you'll develop a clear understanding of what you're making and what you're spending on a regular basis. You'll also need to start budgeting and start thinking about investing and retirement. Then all you'll have to do is actually stick to your plan and believe in it, as well as in yourself. These two things are crucial for your ability to manifest money.

If belief is something you generally struggle with, then writing a positive financial affirmation otherwise known as a money mantra, of some kind could be immensely helpful for you (Sharkey, 2023). The kind of money mantra that you want is one that will quickly remind you of your intentions, much in the same way that the item you've chosen to anchor your intentions in will. In fact, you could consider repeating your mantra to yourself while holding that object in your hand, to make the practice really effective. Some examples of good money mantras to have might be:

- My income offers me unlimited potential and I have unlimited earning opportunities.
- I am financially stable and thriving.
- I am financial free

Repeating your financial affirmation or affirmations to yourself can get you into the right, positive mindset you need to be in to manifest money. Another thing that can make it possible for you to achieve this is examining your financial intentions every day. This can be a great way to both start and end the day and focus your attention and energy on the things that most matter to you. You can even write down your financial intentions on little post-it notes and then paste them around your home. This way, you can get little, uplifting reminders of them every time you open a cupboard and come across one or glance at the ones sticking to the fridge door or the mirror.

The struggle with financial intentions is that losing sight of what is really important for you—that is to say why you're trying to earn more money to begin with—can be all too easy. We live in a rather materialistic world, after all. That is why focusing on your values when setting your intentions and framing them in a way that reflects them is a more effective way of manifesting money than anything else. Keeping a journal about your financial intentions can make this process a great deal easier. A money intentions journal can only refocus your attention on what truly matters to you, but also provide you with a space where you can organize your running thoughts and calm things down. In addition to this, it can become a platform where you can calmly and logically think your way around or through any obstacles that stand in your way and visualize how major a success your efforts will lead you to. It will even give you an avenue where you can start facing your financial fears and bit and edge your way towards taking healthy risks.

Taking Risks and Facing Your Fears

Given everything that you've discovered about the art of manifesting, it should come as no surprise to find out that fear can be a major roadblock for you, if you let it. This is especially true when you consider how your fears can keep you from taking risks, be they financial or not. There is an old saying you may be familiar with: No risk, no reward. It is applicable to all aspects of life, of course, but it is most true where your efforts to earn and manifest money are concerned. There are different kinds of financial risks that you can take in life that will yield different kinds of results. There are high risks that yield high rewards, which might make them worth taking, depending on the situation. There are high risks that yield very low rewards too, which are not all that worth it. Similarly, there are low risks with high rewards—these are the kinds of risks you typically should take—and low risks with low rewards, which you can take or leave again depending on the situation.

The reason you might be afraid of risk taking might be that the ones you took in the past did not pan out. It might also be that you think of risks as "reckless", which they are not or at least they don't have to be (Morin, 2020). When you see risk taking as a "reckless" kind of behavior, you link it intimately with your fear. So, you end up using your level of fear as a gauge as to how risky a decision or behavior is. You cannot accurately gauge risk in this manner, though. What will happen instead is that your fear will keep you from taking the risk before you, making it appear as though it is more dangerous than it is or that the reward it will yield is less than it will be. This is the power that fear can have over you. Add to how the waves of negative energy that fear will send out to the universe and it is easy to see how it can block manifestation.

One solution you can turn to when your fear seems to be getting the better of you is to hit "pause", calm yourself down a little bit, and think through the issue logically. Your deep breathing exercises should help calm you down significantly. Once you can feel your heart and breathing rates settling down, you can start asking yourself questions like:

- What risk or risks will I actually be taking if I do this?
- What rewards do I stand to gain?
- How can I handle things if they don't work out as I want them to?

Answering such questions calmly and objectively will give you a clearer, more honest picture of the risk before you. You'll then be able to properly determine whether it is worth it or not. If you're having trouble answering these questions, you could try exploring them in a journal entry. That way, you'll see all that you stand to gain and lose laid out before you and you might realize that the risk in question is not as catastrophic as your fear made it appear to be.

A second strategy to employ that can alleviate your fears around risk taking behavior is to take steps that can increase your overall chance of success. This can mean any number of things. For example, say that you're considering investing, which can certainly be a risky endeavor. One thing you can do to both lessen your risk of failure and increase your chances of success is to diversify your portfolio. Diversifying your portfolio translates to investing in as many different things as you can. Investing in just a number of different stocks is a good start but it is not really diversifying. Investing in different stocks, bonds, real estate, and mutual funds, for example, is because it spreads out the overall risk you take. That means that should you take a loss in one investment, you gain the possibility and ability to recoup that loss in another investment and make a profit in yet another.

This is just one example of behaviors that can impact the level of risk you want to take. There are many others, which means that you have to consider the risk before you carefully and ask yourself what you can do to lessen it. Writing down the answers to that question is a good starting point. You'll then have to act on them, of course. As you do so, you'll be surprised at how effective your actions were in lessening your fear. Another method that can facilitate this is making sure to take baby steps when you first start taking risks. You have to crawl and walk before you can run for a reason, after all. The key reason here is that taking smaller risks at first can get you used to the idea of taking risks. The more you do something, the less afraid of it you'll become. So, the more you take small risks, the more you'll increase your risk tolerance (Nurow, 2022). Now, you might experience a loss or two with these small risks, but their scale will help you to get used to the occasional loss as well. Once you see that a loss is not as catastrophic or terrifying as you thought it would be, you'll find risk taking behavior gets easier. You'll also be able to learn from the experience and thus ensure that you never repeat it in the future where bigger risks with bigger rewards are concerned.

Fear of failure is obviously a major reason why some people hesitate to take risks. Interestingly enough, fear of success is a major reason as well. This is because a lot of us have developed a core limiting belief over the years: That we are not worthy of achieving the success that we want. That is why imposter syndrome is a thing (*4 Ways to Conquer Your Fears,* 2013). Aside from putting out a lot of negative energy, fear of success can halt your efforts at manifestation in a variety of ways. It can cause you to procrastinate on the things that you need to do, for example, all but guaranteeing failure. It can cause you to avoid your responsibilities altogether. It can result in self-sabotaging behavior and derail all your work and manifestation attempts or even lead to self-destructive patterns of behavior.

The best way to overcome fear of success is to acknowledge that it exists, like how you're supposed to do with other negative feelings you might have. Once acknowledged and labeled, you can start exploring the root causes of your fear. Journaling should help with this as well, since it can be a great place to trace its origins years back, sometimes all the way back to your childhood (Moe, 2021b). Your journal can be somewhere where you can explore what your life would look like if you did not achieve the success you want and manifest the money you want to manifest. For best effect, you want to write in your journal about your fear of success and then read previous entries to review them. You don't have to read all of them, but you should strive to go through at least some. This way, you can start picking up on any behavioral patterns and thought patterns that might be blocking you from both doing the work you need to earn the money you want and manifesting it.

One last and rather fascinating way you can overcome your fear of success is to surround yourself with people who freely take risks. Think of this as exposure therapy. The more you see other people take risks, the more comfortable you'll become taking them yourself. What's more, people who are comfortable with risk taking will likely encourage you to do so as well. This can be a good source of external motivation. While you generally need internal motivation to achieve your goals and ambitions, a little bit of external motivation can be a good thing too. This is something anyone who has ever received praise when they were struggling with something could tell you as much. Outside encouragement can give you just the push you need when you're trying to get yourself to take more financial risks and thus overcome your fear of success, fear or failure, or whatever else is holding you back (Goodman, 2013).

Mimicking Others

The kinds of people you surround yourself with plays a vital role in determining how you behave, what kind of mindset and outlook you display, and how successful you are at manifesting. If you surround yourself with positive people, for example, you end up developing a more positive mindset and outlook too, which reflects in your thoughts, emotions, behavior, and attitude. If, on the other hand, you surround yourself with more negative people, you start adopting a more negative mindset and the behaviors, thoughts, and feelings that go with that. If you want to have manifestation work for you, then you have to make sure to surround yourself with positive people. If you want to manifest money, specifically, then you have to surround yourself with people who are great at earning and manifesting money, are healthy risk takers, and have good financial habits.

You might be skeptical as to how effective surrounding yourself with certain kinds of people would be in altering your mindset and behavior. The thing is, though, this is a widely studied phenomenon in psychology that has been proven again and again in numerous studies. One reason for this is that emotions are literally contagious (Eisenberg et al., 2012). Think about it: When you see someone who is genuinely smiling at you, you get the urge to smile back. When people are laughing around you,

you feel like laughing too, even if you don't know what is so funny. These are probably the most basic examples of how emotions can be contagious. This contagiousness works with more complex emotions as well and is true for both positive and negative emotions. It is therefore one reason why surrounding yourself with positive people is so important for manifestation.

Another reason is that negative people tend to be far more judgmental, pessimistic, and draining. They tend to complain a great deal more than positive people do and their behavior and outlook make it hard for you to remain positive, especially if they start teasing you about your positivity. Faced with such behavior, you become far more likely to think and act negatively as well. Their criticisms and behavior toward you'll likely chip away at your self-confidence too overtime, making you feel a lot more negative too boot. You can imagine the toll all this can take in your mental health and efforts to keep manifesting the things you want, including money.

One last reason the kinds of people you surround yourself with impacts how you think and act is that you become motivated to act like them, whether you realize it or not. Imagine that you're at work and the office is fairly crowded that day. It is an open floor office so you can see what everyone is doing. As you look around, you notice that most of the people there—let us say 75%—are fully concentrating on their work. They're highly motivated, dedicated, and energized. The rest are unmotivated but pretty soon you notice that they start behaving exactly the way the majority of the group is. Not long after that, everyone, including you, is busy working away. Now imagine if the opposite scenario were true and that the majority of the office was slacking off, only appearing to look busy but twiddling their thumbs instead (Chui, 2017). Would the hard working minority then find themselves matching their pace and level of effort after a certain while, even if they are only doing so subconsciously? They certainly would and so would you.

With all this being the case, the undeniable fact of the matter is that you want to surround yourself with people who are good at manifesting money. You similarly want to surround yourself with individuals who have good financial habits and the positive mindsets needed to go with them. Such individuals will be more likely to encourage you to partake in healthy financial habits. They will be more likely to display those habits too so you can mimic and mirror them. Overtime, those behaviors and attitudes you're mirroring will become reflexive and second nature to you. As such, they will support your efforts to manifest money as much as any other aligned action can.

Genuine Charity

Speaking of aligned actions, there is always donating to charity. Giving away money may sound like a rather odd way of earning more money but it cannot be denied that it is a very effective one. This all has to do with the positive energy you send out into the universe by giving to charity or doing charity work. It is also because it makes use of the powers of karma. At its most basic, karma can be defined as the actions you take and the consequences that they have (Felton, 2022). The logic here is simple: Do good and receive good in kind. This is very in keeping with the law of attraction, since the energy you give off is the energy you end up attracting.

This only works, though, if the intentions behind your actions are genuine, as those intentions affect the vibrational frequency of the energy you send to the universe. This is why simply doing good deeds is not enough. You have to believe in what you're doing and want to do it. You have to feel good about what you're doing for your actions to have the effect you want in the world. This is especially true when you're giving money to charity or doing charity work.

There are numerous reasons why genuine charity helps you manifest more money and even abundance and wealth. The first is that it makes the law of attraction work for you. The second is that it pushes you toward adopting an abundance mindset as opposed to a scarcity mindset, which is very helpful in manifesting money, just as it was helpful in manifesting abundance (Brock, 2021). A third reason, of course, is that charity helps you to focus your attention on where it needs to be. This makes you work toward your goal in a more dedicated and motivated way, not to mention with a more positive outlook.

All of this increases your ability to manifest money and you need only look to some of the wealthiest people in the world to see how effective genuine charity can be in manifesting money. Take Bill Gates, for example. We all know how immensely successful Bill Gates is but did you know that Gates has donated $27 million to various charities around the world throughout the course of his professional life (Maurya, 2021)? Did you also know that one of Gates' lifelong missions is to donate 99% of his wealth? How about Warren Buffet, the CEO of Berkshire Hathaway, who has donated around $21 million to charity, on top of giving stocks worth $2.9 billion to the Bill and Melinda Gates Foundation, the Susan Thompson Buffett Foundation, and three other major charitable organizations, so that they can continue doing their good work and keep helping scores of people?

If some of the wealthiest people in the world have recognized the value and necessity of charity work, then odds are, they are onto something and that something is that genuine charity works. Of course, for charity to really work, it must be well-intentioned and sincere, as you may have gathered by the number of times I've stressed the word "genuine" so far. Additionally, charity has to become a regular habit and part of your life. That means that you need to be doing charity work or donating to it on a regular basis (Barrett, 2011). By doing so, you can keep your karmic bank account continually in balance, so to speak. You should also maintain a generally positive attitude about money. I mean, if your opinion about money is that it is corrupting or evil, then you're not going to attract a lot of it, no matter how much you donate to charitable organizations. After all, why would the universe deliver something that you believe will "corrupt" you?

A wonderful side effect of donating and charity work is that it makes you truly appreciate and feel grateful for the things that you have in life. It does so by putting things into perspective and by evoking certain altruistic feelings within you. You can take these effects a step further by practicing gratitude on a regular basis. You've already seen how effective gratitude can be for manifesting wealth and abundance, so is it any wonder that it is effective for manifesting wealth too?

If you want to start giving money to charity, then you need to first decide on what charity you want to help. Examining your values can be a good idea at this point, since it will make finding a charity that aligns with them easier. Say that taking care of the environment is very important for you. Then obviously, an environmentalist charity will be the way to go for you. Alternatively, say that immigration issues are near and dear to your heart. Then you want to look for charities related to that. At this point, you'll probably need to do a little bit of research, unless you know for sure what charity you want to go with. The platform Charity Navigator can be a great help to you in this regard. This website has trust indicators next to each charity it features, which means that you never have to worry that the funds you're donating will be ill-used.

The next thing you need to decide on is how much you're going to donate to charity and whether that sum is going to be given to a single institution or to be divided between multiple different ones (Brock, 2021). Most wealth experts suggest donating 10% of your income to charities. How much you donate is entirely up to you and your circumstances, of course. When you decide how much you want to donate to charity, you'll have to settle on a way to donate too. There are a couple to choose from. You can go with giving circles, which involve community gatherings, donor-advised funds, or private foundations. Then, you just start donating regularly. Over the years, you can adjust and ideally increase how much you donate to charity based on how your income changes.

It may take a while, but the karma that you put into the universe in this way will come back to you in a number of ways, including helping you manifest more money. The more money you'll get, the more you'll need to figure out what to do with it. Finding more charities to give to might be one option, but it is not the only one. While it is important to help others, you should also help yourself to grow and develop. That way, you can create more and greater opportunities for yourself.

Investing in Yourself and in Your Team

Investing in yourself and in your team, for that matter, is one of the surest ways to start manifesting money. This is not just true because it is the kind of habit that helps you develop an abundance and growth mindset. It is also because it expands your skill set and develops skills you already possess. This, in turn, makes you able to go for gig and positions that can bring you more money, since you'll now have the abilities needed to fulfill their responsibilities.

In life, the best thing you can ever invest in is yourself because you have infinite potential. All you need to do is recognize that. A lot of people hesitate to invest in themselves because they either see themselves as not worth the investment or they think that investing in themselves is a selfish thing to do. Neither of these things are true in any way, shape, or form. The former reasoning—that you're not worth investing in—is a kind of limiting belief, one that is the product of a negative mindset. Working to switch from a negative mindset to a positive one should help to dismantle it. The change will not be instantaneous, but the more you practice, say, positive self-talk or hypnosis, for example, the more you'll be able to commit to this world view.

As for the latter thought, dismantling it requires adjusting your perspective a little as well because investing in yourself is one of the least selfish things you can do. While investing in yourself is beneficial for you in a number of ways, it is beneficial for others too. When you invest in yourself, you end up doing things that improve your skills, along with your physical and mental health. By improving your skills, you become a stronger team member at your work, which means you make everyone's lives easier. By improving your physical and mental health, you improve your capacity to be there and support other people. After all, how could you offer someone the moral support they need, for example, if you're going to pieces yourself? In this respect, investing in yourself is very similar to self-care. It can even be considered a form of self-care, when you think about it.

Investing in yourself is also something that people with growth mindsets do, because such individuals recognize that they are not static and unchangeable. Rather, they know that they can always improve their strengths, learn new skills, work on their weaknesses, learn from their mistakes, and improve their intelligence. Thus, they work toward doing these things by investing in themselves. Overall, there are four areas in which you, like other people with growth mindsets, can invest in yourself (Crossett, 2023). These areas are:

- your physical and mental health
- your education
- your relationships
- your ability to develop good habits and break bad ones

If you want to lead a happy and prosperous life, then your physical and mental health are the first things you need to start investing in. Just as you can't be there for other people if you're not feeling well, you can't do much of anything else either. Working while you're sick is pretty hard, if not impossible to do depending on how severe your illness is. That means that manifesting money when you're sick is not all that possible either. Your health is something that gives you the strength you need to take those actions that are necessary to your being able to earn more money. In addition to that, it is what gives you the freedom you need to make choices throughout your everyday life and enjoy the things that you have. Considering all these things, your health needs to be your top priority when you're trying to determine how you should invest in yourself.

Your second priority should be your learning and education. The thing about education is that it does not just end the day you're done with school. You actually learn something new every day, whether you realize it or not and your capacity to learn is boundless. This is something you can and should consciously take advantage of. That way, you can start ingesting the kind of information that can expand your expertise. By investing in your education, you can make yourself far more knowledgeable in your field than you already are. This is something that doctors, for instance, recognize. It is why they constantly read medical articles and new research papers in their free time. That is the only way they can keep up to date on all the new discoveries that are being made in medicine, learn how to utilize them, and incorporate them into their practice. You don't have to be a doctor to invest in your education, especially seeing as we are in the information age. All you need to do is take some time to pursue knowledge, be it through taking online courses, listening to informative podcasts, reading online articles, or something else entirely.

Investing in your relationships is just as important as investing in your education for two reasons. The first is that as human beings we need close relationships and interactions with other people for our mental well-being. Without close relationships, you can become very isolated and your risk of developing a mental health problem of some sort, like depression, increases. This obviously puts you in a more negative frame of mind that is hard to break free from. This both makes it more difficult for you to do the work you need to earn money and keeps you from manifesting money by driving you toward giving off a great deal more negative energy.

As for the second reason why you want to invest in your relationships, that can be summed up with one word: Networking. Networking is an immensely useful business strategy and tool. While your talents and level of expertise are obviously important in a professional context, what kind of network you have can be just as important. In business, things often come down to who you know. Know the right people and you can find the perfect mentor. Know the right people and you can find out about the ideal job opportunities or get introduced to someone you really need to make contact with for the sake of your future career. Surround yourself with the right people with the positive, constructive attitudes and habits for manifesting money and you'll get caught in their positive energies, switch to a mindset that supports it, and start emulating their positive behaviors too, as you have.

Speaking of habits, the kinds of financial habits you develop obviously impact your ability to earn and manifest money. As such, it is important that you identify what kinds of habits that you have. This can be a little tough, at least initially, but it is not impossible to do. The process begins with you making a list of all your financial habits. At this point, you need to write down both your good habits and your bad ones. Once the list is complete, you can take a careful look at each and every item on there and ask yourself how they affect you. Do these habits serve you or not? Do they have any benefits for you? How about any disadvantages? How do these habits make you feel and what needs are they fulfilling? As a most basic example, say that you go shopping anytime you feel stressed. This habit obviously makes you feel good, as in less stressed, by giving you a burst of serotonin. However, it probably is not very good for your bank account and it is only a temporary solution for stress. Hence, it is an unhealthy coping mechanism and habit that you need to change.

Having identified the habits that you'd like to change, like stress shopping, your next order of business is to work on replacing the habit. Going back to the shopping example, the root cause of this habit is stress. This means that you'll not be able to drop this habit if you don't find some other, healthier, and more long term way to cope with your stress. After you've identified a good stress coping mechanism, you can work on replacing shopping with it anytime you feel your anxiety level climbing and feel the urge to head to a store. Again, this will not be easy initially because habits are powerful things. When you develop a habit, your brain creates new neural pathways for executing it. The more you engage in a habit, the stronger those pathways become and the more reflexive your habit gets to be (Blount, 2016).

This is why you can engage in your habits without having to consciously think about them. When you work to replace one habit with another, you're essentially trying to create new neural pathways that can take the place of the old ones. While this process works, it takes a while for those old neural pathways to weaken and then disappear, and new ones to form and become more defined. Replacing your habits, then, is a process that you have to undertake with determination and dedication. Otherwise, it will not work out.

Investing in yourself in these various ways can have a great many benefits to offer you. The most obvious of these is that they expand your expertise and strengths, allowing you to get to positions where you can earn and manifest a lot more money. Other benefits that investing in yourself can offer you are that it:

- opens up new avenues for career advancement, taking you a step closer to success
- makes it possible for you to reach your goals much faster, financial or otherwise
- keeps you up to date with the latest developments in your chosen field
- sharpens your focus as you work toward your goals
- increases your self-confidence, competence, and self-esteem levels, thereby helping you send more positive energy into the world

- strengthens both your physical and mental health
- makes you more resilient for turbulent times that may occur in the future

A final benefit that investing in yourself can offer you is that it can lower your stress and anxiety levels significantly, thanks to how it affects things like your sense of competence and self-esteem. In general, you want to have lower levels of stress and anxiety since these two feelings can be important money blocks. They can also cause you to worry unnecessarily about money, preventing you from spending and enjoying what you earn in the process, which is hardly helpful for manifestation purposes.

Enjoying What You Earn

As you have throughout the course of this chapter, spending money is not inherently a bad thing. In fact, if you want to manifest money, you do have to spend it. True, you have to spend what you earn wisely, but you have to spend it nonetheless. You can do this by investing in yourself, donating to charity, spoiling yourself every once in a while, and spending time with your friends and family when the activities that you're getting up to are within your budget. Such things can significantly boost your happiness and overall satisfaction with your life, making you send out more positive energy into the world.

The trick to spending money is to do it while adhering to your financial plans and in a way that brings you joy. That way you can attract even more money into your life to do even more things that make you feel this way. The question you have to answer for yourself is "What brings me joy?" Everyone derives joy from different things. Some people love traveling, for instance. Others are happiest at home, curling up on the sofa with a good, new book and a cup of tea. Still others love going out regularly with friends and attending interesting events. The point here is that if you want to really enjoy what you learn, you have to figure out what you enjoy doing. Similarly, you should figure out the things that are most important to you. This way, you can make sure that whatever you spend your money on will ultimately align with your values.

Once you've figured out what you enjoy doing, you'll have to factor these things into your financial goals and plans. If you enjoy traveling, for instance, then a good short term financial goal to set for yourself might be to "Save up enough money to go to Bali this year." After setting your enjoyment-oriented financial goals, you'll be able to make them a part of your financial plan. You'll be able to figure out how to make room for this new goal in your budget and work toward meeting it accordingly.

When it comes to enjoying what you earn, the core rule to remember is that you have to account for your spending in your financial plans. Otherwise, the money you earn will lose its meaning and thus, a great part of its true value for you. It will cease to bring you enjoyment, which will prevent you from feeling good and positive about your ability to earn. That will become a mental and emotional block for manifesting money in and of itself. If enjoying the money you earn is something that you personally struggle with, then what you need to do is take action to replace this line of thinking. You can achieve this by turning to methods such as positive self-talk and positive affirmations. Actually, a very effective method that you can turn to, which uses the power of positive affirmations to great effect, is the 369 Method. A startling tool that can enable you to change your mindset from a negative to a positive one, the 369 Method can help you to manifest anything your heart desires, not just money, as you'll discover in the subsequent chapter.

Chapter 7:
The 369 Method

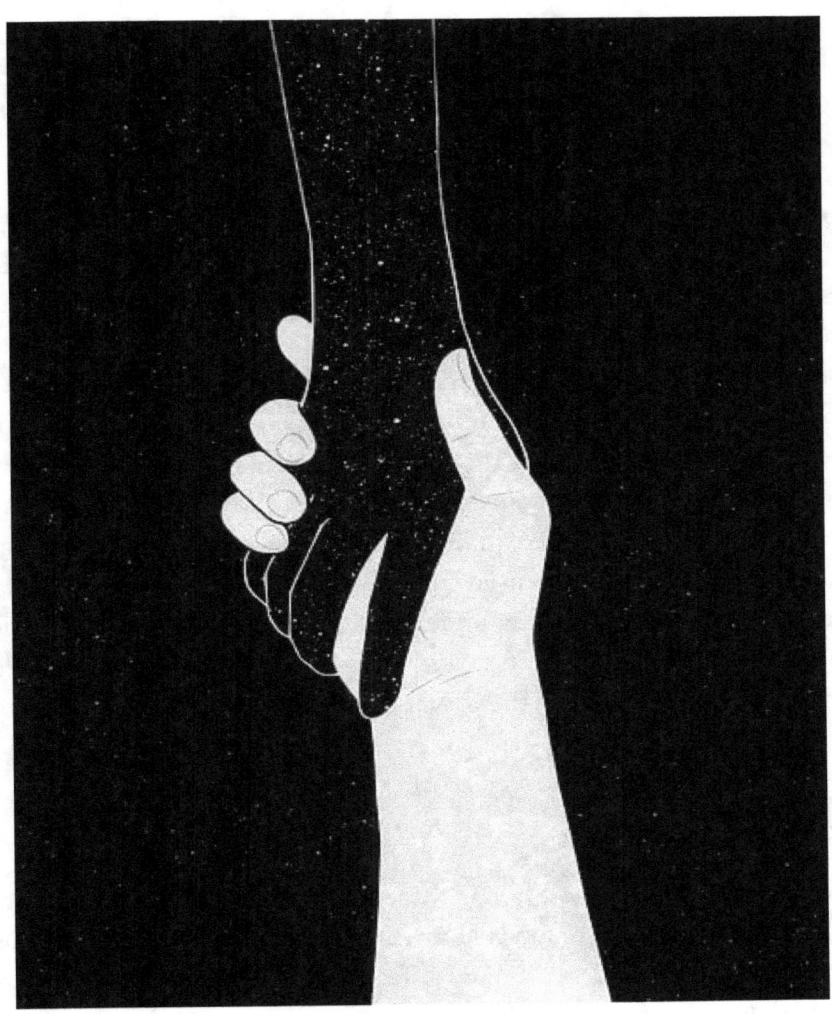

If you only knew about the magnificence of the 3, 6, and 9, you'd have the key to the universe. –Nikola Tesla

A great many manifestation techniques make use of the power of writing, as you may have noticed. This is because the act of writing something down makes it more real and visible for our brains. It is not surprising, then, that one of the most powerful manifestation techniques we have, the 369 Method, relies heavily on the power of writing. It also relies on the power of repetition. Repetition is another important manifestation tool because the more you repeat something, the easier it is to remember it. The things you repeat effectively get stuck in your mind and over time, become things that you internalize. Repeat the right, positive things, and this can influence your mindset, actions, and ability to manifest that which you want.

So, what exactly is the 369 Method? Well, the idea it is based around is fairly simple. You write the things you want to manifest but not just the once. Instead, you write each of them down thrice in the morning, six times in the afternoon, and nine times at night. Why those numbers, specifically? This is because the numbers "3", "6", and "9" are known to hold special powers. These numbers can be so powerful, in fact, that their effectiveness has been recognized by some of the smartest, most influential people throughout history. Take the inventor Nikola Tesla, for example, who invented things like the Tesla coil and the rotating magnetic field, which are used in a number of machines and bits of technology that are vital parts of our lives. Tesla was a recognized genius in his time—meaning the 19th and 20th centuries—and he wholeheartedly believed in the power of these numbers. So much so that he is known to have said, "If you only knew the magnificence of the 3, 6, and 9, you'd have the key to the universe" (*Guide to Manifestation Methods: 369 Method*, 2022).

Seeing as the 369 Method brings these numbers together, it can be said that *it* is the key to the universe, then. These numbers matter because they each mean and represent different yet very important things. According to numerology, the number "3" represents your connection to the universe, as well as your ability to express yourself creatively. Number "6" represents your inner strength and the harmony you achieve both internally and externally. As for "9", this number represents your ability to let go of things that either no longer serve you or that hinder you and thus, transform. In other words, it represents your rebirth (Regan, 2021).

If you know nothing about numerology and therefore don't have any real idea how credible it is, then one thing you should be aware of is that it is not a new belief system. Rather, it is a kind of science that has been around for centuries and ancient civilizations across the globe used to use it pretty frequently (Buchanan, 2016). In fact, numerology was created in Ancient Greece, 2,500 years ago, by a man called Pythagoras. This was the same guy who invented the Pythagorean Theorem, which you might remember from high school. He wasn't the only one though, as ancient China, Indian, and Chaldean civilizations had their own, much older versions of numerology. Regardless of its country of origin, numerology is based on the idea that every number and letter in the world has its own, unique vibrational frequency. So, by tapping into these frequencies, you can manifest things that have similar vibrational frequencies. So, the reason why number "3" represents your connection to the universe is that its vibrational frequency is similar to that. The same logic applies to numbers "6" and "9", naturally.

Over the years, a lot of people have become aware of this fact thanks to social media, where the 369 Method suddenly went viral. A widely shared hashtag was created for the practice—#369method—and it really took off on Tik Tok. Last time I checked, this hashtag had over 214 million views and that figure was only climbing (Tempera & Talbert, 2022). Most of these videos were testimonials. Influences who had tried it were taking to social media in droves, it seems, to sing the method's praises and describe how it helped them manifest their heart's desires. What people remarked about the most was how quickly the 369 Method made things happen. When you look at the method and compare it with other tools and techniques, it is easy to see that it is one of the more speedy devices you can turn to. While manifestation can take some time, the 369

Method is amazing at speeding things along and thus, making sure you get whatever you want in record time (Fellizar, 2022).

The 369 Method was created by Karin Yee, who is a very well-known Law of Attraction guru, and who started looking into the power of these numbers after reading what Tesla had to say about them (*What Is the 369 Manifestation Method*, 2022). The 369 Method, as Karin conceived of it, is not just about repeating a chosen phrase or affirmation a number of times. There are certain guidelines that you should follow and adhere to as well. By doing so, you can increase the effectiveness of the 369 Method and speed it up even more.

How Does it Work?

Before you can kick the 369 Method off, you have to choose a phrase or affirmation to do it with. You can choose multiple such phrases or affirmations, if you'd like, so long as they are positive and specific. If you're going with a phrase, then it must be something that clearly expresses the thing you're trying to manifest. Assuming this is going to be your first ever attempt at utilizing the 369 Method, then you should just choose the one for now. That way, you can really give it your whole focus. As for which of the many possibilities that are probably flickering in and out of your mind, right now, try to go with the one that feels or is most important to you at this moment in time. After you've chosen your phrase or affirmation, evaluate it with an objective eye. Is it as specific as it can be? Remember, manifestation loves specificity. While you're at it, is it expressed and framed in a positive way? If not, then that is something you want to and should fix.

When you feel confident that you've the right phrase or affirmation, you can move onto your next step, which is take a notebook—you can have a dedicated one just for this practice—and start writing. Now, it is important that you start from a place of gratitude when you start writing. This will ensure that you bring the right energy and attitude to the practice. It will also make it easier for you to focus not on what you don't have but what you do. Filled with a sense of gratitude, you'll be able to manifest that which you want through this practice much more quickly.

One thing to keep in mind when you're writing down your phrase or affirmation is that the act of writing a single phrase shouldn't take you more than 17 seconds. This is actually a rule that you should abide by anytime you're working on positive affirmations for yourself and it is quite literally called the 17 Second Rule. The 17 Second Rule was created by author and law of attraction guru Esther Hicks. More specifically, it was created by the group of non-physical entities that she channels and refers to as Abraham-Hicks (Wong, 2021b). Why 17 seconds? It is because those 17 seconds actually activate the vibrational frequency of the thought that is on your mind, which is your positive phrase or affirmation during the course of this practice. For the record, an affirmation that takes exactly 17 seconds to write is one that is about two sentences-long.

Going back to 369 Method itself, when you are writing your phrase or affirmation, you should focus on the gratitude that getting the thing you're trying to manifest will bring into your life. You should similarly write with as much feeling as you possibly can. As a rule, the more genuine you're when repeating an affirmation or practicing positive self-talk, the more you'll believe in what you are saying. Thus, the faster the thing you want will become your reality. A great way to do this is to imagine yourself receiving the thing you're trying to manifest as you are writing your affirmation in your journal. This will release all the right energies and vibrational frequencies into the universe (Jackson, 2021).

After that, all you have to do is write thrice a day, meaning three times in the morning, six times in the afternoon, and nine times at night. Let us be honest, in the grand scheme of this, doing so will not take too much of your time, even if you lead a busy lifestyle. You have to do this every day for the 369 Method to actually work. There are a couple of other things you can do to increase its effectiveness, too. You can, for instance, do your evening right before you go to bed. This way, you can conclude your day with the right vibrational frequency. You can and should also keep up the practice for 33 days in a row, since that would use the powers of three to the max, what with 3x3 equaling 9 and 3+3 equaling 6.

Another thing you can try to boost the technique's effectiveness is to trust that you'll receive the very thing you're manifesting before your 33 days are up. This strengthens the positive energy you're sending out into the universe, often ensuring you get what you want unexpectedly quickly. The key word there, however, is "often". There may be times when what you're manifesting comes your way a bit more slowly. There may also be times when you don't receive that which you were manifesting, despite the fact that 33 days have gone by. You shouldn't despair or give up hope in cases like these. Just because you haven't gotten what you're manifesting as quickly as you hoped, does not mean you'll not get it. It just means that getting it is going to take you a little bit longer than anticipated and that is fine.

Having said that, if manifestation is taking a long time, you may want to hit pause and take a closer look at the mindset you get into as you are using the 369 Method. The thing is, if you keep thinking "This is never going to work" as you write down your affirmations morning, noon, and night, then you're right in that what you're trying to manifest will never come to pass. But that will not be because the method does not work, It will be because you're not in the right frame of mind for it. It is normal to sometimes struggle with doubt and even self-doubt. However, it is important that you physically take a step back from what you're doing, hit pause, and question the thoughts that are running through your mind in such instances. Say that you really are thinking "This will never work." A great way to change this line of thinking is to question the evidence, which is a strategy you may remember from earlier chapters. So, what evidence do you have that supports this thought? What evidence do you have that goes against it? Is this a real, undeniable fact or is it merely a belief and one that you can change, at that?

An interesting strategy that can help you at this stage is to use breathing exercises or even meditation practices while you question your beliefs. These can be used when you are using the 369 Method as well (Tempera & Talbert , 2022). This way, you can all but guarantee you'll slip into a more open-minded and relaxed state, which is very conducive for manifesting. It can make you far more open to receiving the things that you want and help you match it vibrationally.

Chapter 8:

Positive Psychology

If positive psychology teaches us anything, it is that all of us are a mixture of strengths and weaknesses. No one has it all and no one lacks it all. –Chris Peterson

Aside from being a term that you've encountered multiple times throughout this book, positive psychology is a form of psychology that studies the things that make life worth living (Ackerman, 2018). To that end, positive psychology focuses on three specific things, these being:

- positive experiences like love or happiness
- positive traits to have or states to be in, such as compassion
- positive institutions, which apply these positive experiences, traits, and states into their very organization

Positive psychology is obviously deeply connected to manifestation. Before we dive deeper into the "how" of the matter and what positive psychology is at its care, we must first understand where it comes from. The roots of positive psychology can be traced all the way back to the Ancient Greeks, whose philosophers, like Aristotle, loved studying happiness and the good life, as they put it (Al Taher, 2015). However, positive psychology as we know it today, did not come into existence until the 20th century. The movement did not really start taking shape until the 1990s, in fact. Until then, most brands of psychology focused on diseases, disorders, and dysfunctions. There was no branch of psychology, you see, that studies the positives of human experience and attitudes, like joy and happiness.

Since positive psychology is a relatively new field, it took a little bit of time for it to catch on and to even develop a vocabulary of its own. By 2004, however, it had succeeded at doing both, taking psychologists, sociologists, social psychologists, and various other researchers by storm. Over the years, positive psychology came up with some key findings and core beliefs that a lot of practices, such as positive self-talk and affirmations, are built on.

What is Positive Psychology?

Positive psychology has 10 core beliefs that form the basis of its studies and stresses that human beings have three key strengths. The 10 beliefs that the approach is built on are that:

- Most human beings are inherently happy.

- Happiness is the cause of all good things in life and is not the result of things like success, victory, or other "good" outcomes. Rather, it is the other way around, which means that happy people are able to make good things happen.

- Most human beings are pretty resilient and often more so than they think. As such, they can bounce back from failure, mistakes, obstacles, and other setbacks.

- There are three things that can act as buffers against the negative effects that can come with setbacks and disappointment, these being good relationships with others, happiness, and strengths of character.

- Belief matters as people who have some kind of belief system tend to be happier and are able to cope better with stress than people who don't.

- Money does contribute to a person's well-being on a small scale but it is able to buy one's happiness when you spend it on other people.

- A life that is filled with meaning trumps one that is about pleasure.

- A good day can be characterized as one where you feel connected to others, autonomous, and competent.

- The good life is something you can learn to live.

- Your heart matters as much as your mind, which means that traits such as compassion and empathy are just as important as things like your critical thinking skills, if not more so (Walters, 2020).

That positive psychology is built on such beliefs means that it supports the use of positive traits and approaches in achieving different, desired outcomes. The idea here is that things like disorders stem from the absence or excess of the positive traits that these beliefs are built on. It is also that things like your well-being and happiness are just as important and worth studying as typical mental health disorders, which traditional psychology prioritizes studying.

How about the core strengths of a human being that positive psychology stresses that we all have? These strengths are forgiveness, gratitude, and humility. The first of these, forgiveness, is an essential strength for your ability to maintain long term, harmonious relationships with others, as well as with yourself. It can be vital for dealing with difficult emotions like self-loathing or guilt, even resentment, which can lead to hatred—again, toward others or toward the self—if you let it fester. If such emotions can be thought of as "wounds", then forgiveness could be considered the healing balm. The problem with forgiveness is that most people find it hard to do. This is because human beings have a penchant for retaliation and revenge, which are survival tactics left over to us from the stone age days. These used to be survival tactics because the primitive world that our ancestors used to live in necessitated living by a "If you want to survive, hit someone back harder when they hit you" kind of mentality (Lopez, 2019). Obviously, we no longer live in such a dog-eat-dog world, at least not to that degree. Yet we still have the instinct to "hit back" whenever conflict arises and this instinct can cause us to hurt the people around us and then come to regret it.

Without forgiveness, your instinct for retaliation often leads to one of two things: revenge and negative reciprocity. Revenge is causing someone to suffer for suffering's sake, in retaliation for some type of hurt that has been inflicted on you. Usually, the hurt that you inflict in retaliation is disproportional to what has been done to you. The driving emotion behind revenge is hatred. They are further fueled by the idea that someone else's existence will eventually cause you harm. As for negative reciprocity, this entails retaliating to someone who has hurt you as well, but it is more proportional. In this instance, you only hurt the person before you as much as they have hurt you. Unlike revenge, negative reciprocity is fueled not by hatred, but by anger. Since it is more proportional than revenge, the possibility of repairing a relationship afterward still exists in negative reciprocity. It really does not, however, in revenge.

While negative reciprocity is mildly healthier than revenge, it is not by any means healthy or healing for you or your relationships. Forgiveness, however, is. Forgiving someone or yourself requires that you resist these two impulses that you have, which is why it can be rather difficult. Yet it is worth the trouble you go through for it, as positive psychology has discovered. This is due to several reasons, one being that when you forgive others you effectively end up forgiving yourself. When you hold a grudge against someone for hurting you, you sometimes end up getting mad at yourself for "letting it happen" (Brenner, 2020). You turn to self-blame, self-criticism, and self-anger, which does a number on your self-confidence, as well as cause you to get caught in loops of negative thinking.

Forgiving others prevents this from happening because you simultaneously allow yourself to forgive yourself. It enables you to let go of feelings like resentment and start the healing process. It makes it possible for you to think more positively and work toward reconciliation too. Another benefit of forgiveness is that it is freeing. You see, forgiveness effectively allows you to take your power back by letting you take all the emotion and energy you've invested in someone and redistribute it in a more positive way. You may reinvest that energy on that person, of course, or you can invest some of it in them and the rest in something else that is positive for your emotional and psychological health and well-being. This naturally improves the vibrational frequency that you tap into and send out to the universe.

Forgiveness helps you stop playing the victim too. This is vital if you want to get into a positive mindset and put out a more positive energy out there. When you get used to playing the victim, you allow negative feelings and the negative energy that they bring to control your thoughts, actions, and decisions. This happens even when you pretend that nothing's wrong and that everything has gone back to normal. That negative energy still remains, polluting your mind, interrupting your attempts at manifestation, and souring your relationships.

A very interesting benefit of forgiveness is that it is really rather good for your health. When you get swept up by negative emotions, you lose a great deal of energy. You become more stressed and anxious, on top of all the other negative things you're already feeling. As a result, your mental health deteriorates, making it more likely for you to develop some kind of mental health disorder like generalized anxiety disorder or depression. Forgiveness prevents this from happening while looking out for your physical health too. When you're unable to forgive people, you become more stressed, as was said. That means a lot more cortisol ends up pumping through your system than normal. Those high levels of cortisol keep your heartbeat and breathing rates up and your blood pressure levels elevated. In the short term, this is not too major an issue but in the long term it can take a heavy toll on your body. Chronic stress—meaning stress that you feel all of the time—can thus tire out your heart muscles, arteries, and even cause you to develop respiratory issues.

Forgiveness is a character strength, according to positive psychology, but it is not one that you're either born with or not. None of the character strengths that positive psychology emphasizes that we have are. Instead, they are all things you can learn to adopt, develop, and get better at (Enright, 2015). Getting better at forgiving others and yourself starts with making a commitment to doing no harm, since both revenge and negative reciprocity are built on the idea of doing harm unto others. This will require some conscious effort on your part to mind your words, thoughts, and actions, especially when you're experiencing powerful, negative emotions like anger. This will be a little hard, but It will get easier to do once you start acknowledging the hurt that you're experiencing as well. When we get hurt, one of our gut reactions is to deny or hide it, as if we can will the pain away by doing so. We can't. What can make the hurt go away or at least lessen to a manageable degree is to acknowledge that it is there and try to understand where it is coming from.

Say that you're really angry at a friend. You have two options in this case. Either you can launch accusations at them and get into a full blown fight or you can acknowledge your anger and ask yourself what it is trying to tell you. Why is your friend insisting you share something private that you said you did not want to talk about with them, angering you so much? It might take you a little while to figure out the answer to that question, so I'll just give it to you straight: It is because your friend is not respecting your boundaries by doing so, which makes you feel hurt and maybe even unsafe. When you figure out why you're feeling hurt and angered in the face of a certain kind of behavior, you become able to communicate it. In this case, you gain the ability to explain to your friend that they are crossing a boundary and that they need to stop. Nine times out of ten, your friend will hear you and back off and it will turn out that they hadn't realized what they were doing was actually hurting or bothering you.

Understanding what you're going through and communicating it to people makes forgiving them infinitely easier. So does working to develop empathy, which is a major part of positive psychology, as you'll recall. Scientists have discovered that when you actively start thinking about forgiving someone, the part of your brain that is responsible for your ability to empathize with people becomes activated. Empathy is a major part of forgiveness as it makes it possible for you to understand other people's perspectives and where they are coming from. If you are arguing with someone, for example, empathy can help you see that whatever hurt they inflicted was not intentional. Having realized that, you can let go of things more easily and focus on repairing your relationship, while communicating your feelings and needs instead of getting into a shouting match.

True, things don't always go that well. Sometimes it can be hard to forgive someone, especially if they have hurt you a lot and at least were partially aware that they were doing so. In such cases, it is important to remember that forgiveness does not mean forgetting. It also does not mean going back to the way your relationship was before you were hurt. Relationships can change and evolve and the energy you invest in them can change as well, after all. Another thing you need to remember when facing such a situation is that forgiveness is less about the person before you and more about yourself. It is about your wanting to let go of negative emotions like resentment to keep them from affecting your mindset and energy. To achieve this you can always turn to some of your other strengths. Patience, for example, can be a fantastic helper when you're working toward forgiveness. Humility, which is another character strength you want to have, can be too.

Speaking of other character strengths, gratitude is one too. Perhaps you've already come to realize this, given how big a role gratitude plays in the manifestation process and even techniques such as the 369 Method. To recap very quickly, gratitude is the thankfulness and appreciation you feel and express for the gifts or benefits that you receive in life (Walters, 2020). It has an array of psychological, emotional, and physical benefits to offer you, which is why it plays a starring role in positive psychology. Off the top of my head, gratitude, like forgiveness, improves your physical health. According to one study, grateful people usually experience fewer aches and pains across their bodies (Morin, 2015). While there is a psychological component to this, it is likely also related to how grateful people tend to take better care of themselves. They tend to eat healthier, for one, and exercise regularly, since they are grateful for the body, health, and mobility that they have and want to look after them well.

As for psychological health, gratitude obviously improves this as well. It does so by reducing the amount of negative and thus, toxic emotions that you feel on a regular basis. In the process, it reduces your risk of developing depression or other similar mental health issues, and increases their happiness levels. The social impact that gratitude bears is partly responsible for this. Human beings are social creatures. We need genuine human interaction and good, trusting relationships to be happy. Having close friends that we can rely on actively increases our happiness and well-being. Being grateful strengthens your ability to meet new people and make new friends. It makes you have more pleasant, daily interactions, which have the potential to bloom into friendships or other types of relationships in the long run.

Meanwhile, practicing gratitude improves the quality and duration of your sleep. You don't even have to do a lot to enjoy this benefit that this character strength has to offer you. Writing in a gratitude journal for just 15 minutes a day can help you sleep better and longer without any issues. This naturally improves your mental health—no one's exactly happy when they are sleep deprived, as anyone who has ever pulled an all-nighter would know—and it increases your mental resilience. Overcoming obstacles and going through stressful situations is much less easy to do and bear when gratitude is a part of your life.

Finally, gratitude increases your sense of self-esteem. It makes you far less likely to compare yourself to others, which is a good thing considering how badly such comparisons can affect you. They can make you envy and resent clothes, for example, thereby messing with your energy and even damaging your relationships, especially if the person you envy is a friend. Overall, gratitude makes you see your strengths a whole lot more clearly, which makes you trust in your abilities more and appreciate yourself more. This increases your sense of competence, and before you know it, you are exuding confidence, just as you should.

Your final character strength is humility. A lot of people misunderstand humility, because they think that it is synonymous to underappreciating or undervaluing yourself. This is not the case. A more accurate definition of humility would be having a clear and true understanding and perception of your strengths, abilities, and achievements, while being able to acknowledge your imperfections, mistakes, and failures (Walters, 2020). All of these qualities are essential to maintaining a positive mindset and manifesting the things you want. Perhaps this is why humility has a number of benefits to offer you as well. For instance, humility is known to increase your ability to empathize with others and practice compassion (Blain, 2022). Hence, it is better for fostering good relationships with good people. It makes people less self-absorbed and broadens their view and understanding of themselves. Practicing humility, then, makes you more self-aware. At the same time, it broadens your understanding of the world, ensuring that you become far more open minded than you otherwise could have.

Becoming more humble requires working to gain a more thorough understanding of yourself, which in turn requires spending some time doing some soul searching, otherwise known as self-reflection. Meditation and journaling could be excellent practices for this, as can asking other people for feedback, so long as you are open to it. Acknowledging other people's abilities and accomplishments by giving praise where it is due can help you become more humble too. By doing this, you can develop a clearer view of other people and take the focus off of yourself for a little bit. The key to remember here is that you neither want to be overly egotistical nor a pushover. Acknowledging your own abilities, while important, does not mean ignoring or undervaluing those of others. On the flip side, acknowledging other people's abilities does not mean undervaluing or denying your own or comparing yourself to other people. So long as you strive to walk this line, you'll only get better and better at practicing humility until it, like all your other character strengths, becomes second nature to you.

The Building Blocks of Well-Being

By working to develop these three character strengths, you can take some major steps toward leading a happy life and improving your well-being. This is because these three strengths help you develop the building blocks you need to achieve a happy life. According to positive psychology there are five such building blocks (Ackerman, 2018). They are:

- positive emotions
- engagement
- relationships
- meaning
- accomplishment

The power of positive emotions in increasing your happiness, improving your physical and mental well-being, and helping you to manifest the things you want is undeniable. The more you're able to be in the moment and tap into these positive emotions, the more positive energy you'll start giving off, and the better off you'll be. Tapping into your positive emotions becomes easier to do when you prioritize another important building block in positive psychology: engagement. Engagement means being so absorbed in what you're doing that you start enjoying it enough to lose track of time. That engagement is important for your well-being makes a lot of sense, when you think about it. If you're not engaged in the work you have do every day, then at best you'll end up being very bored and at worst, your days will feel as though they are grinding by at a torturously slow pace.

Your third building block is relationships. Obviously, this refers to good and positive relationships, as opposed to negative or toxic ones. When you form positive, deep, and meaningful connections with people, you give your mental health a major boost. You feel more connected to the world around you and more motivated to be an active part of it. In the process, you end up striving to find greater meaning in your life, which is yet another one of our building blocks. You can search for greater meaning in your life in a variety of different ways. Dedicating yourself to a cause that you believe in is one way. Doing something you love is another. Pursuing a lifestyle that aligns with your core values is yet another. There are any number of ways you can find meaning in your life. You can explore these ways by questioning what is important to you and then taking aligned action to realize those things.

Meaning is the kind of building block that goes almost hand in hand with accomplishment. Accomplishment, which can alternatively be called achievement, is your ability to meet your goals and better yourself in the ways that you want to. Pursuing a sense of accomplishment, which you can do by defining success means to you and going after it, is the only real way you can live a good life as your own, authentic self. What does leading a "good" life really mean, though? To understand that, we have to take a closer look at the benefits that positive psychology has to offer you.

Benefits of Positive Psychology

Having discussed the benefits of forgiveness, gratitude, and humility at length, we would be remiss not to touch upon the ones associated with positive psychology, of which there are many. First among these is how adhering positive psychology is a terrific way to find greater meaning in life (Heston, 2020). When you work to develop the character strengths that positive psychology outlines and to adopt its building blocks as the pillars of your life, you find greater purpose in life too. This sense of purpose turns into a kind of jet fuel for you, one that can motivate you significantly and help you to get through challenging and stressful times, along with many obstacles thrown in your way. It pushes you to do your best at all times and ensures that your productivity levels do not go down.

In keeping with that, positive psychology increases your resilience. You have come across the word "resilience" a couple of times throughout this book already. To define the word a little more concretely, resilience is your ability to cope with anything and everything that life throws your way (Fontane Pennock, 2017). Being a resilient person means being able to adapt to a variety of circumstances while retaining your positive outlook, regulate your emotions better, and have a more positive view of yourself. Positive psychology makes you more resilient because the skills and traits it supports helps you to see your strengths better. This increases your self-confidence and self-esteem.

As a general rule, you want to be a confident individual with a high level of self-esteem. The more you value yourself, you see, the more you believe in yourself and the more you are able to achieve. This has been proven in multiple studies over the years and is clearly supported by the law of attraction. What's more, when you have high levels of self-confidence, you attract more people your way, which means you end up forming more and better relationships and friendships. Confidence is like a lighthouse for ships in this regard. Another benefit that positive psychology has to offer you makes itself known in how much stronger it makes those very relationships.

If you remain unconvinced about the importance of having good, strong relationships in your life, then you should know that there is a legitimate correlation between longevity and having a community to call your own. This connection was revealed through a study that was conducted at Harvard University and lasted for 80 years. The study, which began in 1938, meaning while the Great Depression was going on, revealed that there is an immediate correlation between how good your health is and how happy you are in the relationships that you are in (Mineo, 2017).

The study further revealed that it is how many close relationships you have and how close to people you really that affects your level of happiness in life, as opposed to how much money you have. This finding proves one of the core beliefs of positive psychology, as you might have noticed.

Since positive psychology improves your relationships, it is understandable that it would improve your work relationships and work environment too. For starters, it ensures that you forge better relationships with your co-workers, which makes for a much less toxic and far more collaborative environment to be in. Beyond that, it improves your and your co-workers' motivations and makes it easier for everyone to adopt a more positive outlook. All this results in better, that is to say friendlier, warm, and more respectful interactions between both co-workers and employees and clients. Finally, it creates the kind of space wherein employees can actually feel like they are valued by their employers and co-workers alike, which is why they tend to get more motivated when positive psychology is implemented in the workplace.

One often overlooked but no less important benefit of positive psychology is that it helps you to distance yourself from toxic positivity, which is a thing (Ethans, 2022). Many people believe that practicing positive psychology means you have force yourself to be positive all of the time. As such, they repress or ignore any negative thoughts and feelings that they have and don't allow themselves to simply be and exist as they are. Not only is this not what positivity truly is; it is the kind of belief that can damage your mental and physical well-being significantly. Ultimately, it can result in you spiraling into a far more negative mindset than you wanted to be in and experiencing significant difficulties as a result (Dillard et al., 2009). This is why this belief has been dubbed toxic positivity.

Toxic positivity sadly seems to be on the rise lately, despite the obvious dangers that it brings with it. The good news is that true positivity, as it is defined in positive psychology, can help you to beat it back. This can allow you to start truly valuing and validating your emotions and experiences, even when they are more negative (Ethans, 2022). We have negative emotions for a reason and that reason is usually that the emotion you're feeling is trying to tell you something. With true positivity you can stop repressing what you're feeling and start listening, then learning from it instead. You can become a more authentic version of yourself, without feeling the need to repress any parts of you. You can regulate your emotions more and process them properly.

Earlier in this book, you encountered many different ways to manifest money, wealth, and abundance. These ways almost always entailed changing your outlook on these concepts and the value that they had. This might sound like a tall order for some, but it gets easier to do when you adhere to positive psychology and pursue true positivity. This is because these two things improve your very relationship with money, making it much healthier than it was. In general, you want to have a healthy relationship with money and with our personal finances. Obviously, you need money to live, but that does not mean it should become a toxic entity that controls your life. Rather, it should be something that improves your life but does not determine how happy you are in it. Positive psychology can ensure that this is the case through a multitude of ways, as you've seen. From dismantling the sense of guilt when spending money to making you a more giving and thus generous person and driving you to value your life experiences more, it can ensure that you have a well-balanced and good relationship with your bank account.

Having discovered all this, the fact that genuine positivity helps you to improve upon the strengths you already possess should be expected. After all, positivity supports a growth mindset, which is something you want to possess as you move forward in life. To begin with, positivity can actually make you see your strengths. This can be a startling experience, especially if you've grown used to ignoring, denying, or undervaluing them. At the same time, it can make you focus on those strengths, thereby allowing you to sharpen them however you'd like. A great way to improve your strengths is to ask yourself what you love to do—strengths don't necessarily mean things you're good at, as you'll remember, but include things that you enjoy doing too. Focusing on these is bound to help you get better at them, but also to lead a happier, more confident life, which is what we all want at our very core.

Enjoying at least some of these benefits, if not all of them, is a great sign that you're practicing positive psychology and are generally an optimistic kind of person. There are some more obvious signs that you have an optimistic mindset (Scott, 2019b) such as:

- expecting things to work out for the best

- feeling as though you'll succeed in life, even when you're faced with challenges

- feeling like good things are waiting for you in the future

- being able to think of good things and see the silver lining of things, even when the going gets tough and when something challenging or more negative happens

- feeling grateful for all that you have in your life, no matter what circumstances you're living through

- always looking for new opportunities and ways to make the best of the opportunities that you have

- taking responsibility for your failures and mistakes without dwelling on them and letting them drag you down

- not allowing one bad experience to mar your expectations for the future

If these are things that apply to you and your life, then clearly you are a more optimistic person. If, on the other hand, they're qualities that you'd like to have but don't really possess, then it might be time to work on developing a more positive mindset. Luckily, there are a myriad of ways you can do this. One of these is a method called cognitive restructuring, which essentially is a way to reprogram your mind so that you can shift your mindset and look at a situation from a different perspective (Morin, 2019). That means that it is a technique you can use to shift from a negative mindset to a more optimistic one.

How to Be More Positive

The technique kicks off when you identify which situations or circumstances trigger negative moods, emotions, and thoughts for you. When you catch yourself in a negative mood or having a negative thought, you quickly assess how you're feeling at that precise moment and try to define it as concretely as you can. Concurrently, you try to determine which negative thoughts you're having in association with those feelings and in response to the situation that you are in. Then, you turn to your old friend: questioning the evidence. Yes, this technique is actually a part of cognitive restructuring and is widely used by therapists. As part of the technique, you question whether the thoughts you're having are real and what evidence you have both support and refute them. Once you figure out the "truth" of the matter, you focus on the objective facts and these will more than likely be refuting those negative thoughts you were having. As such, they will both be more realistic and positive for you.

An additional technique you can use to become more optimistic is to accept that sometimes disappointment is inevitable (Shain, 2020). It seems odd to say that accepting the inevitability of the occasional disappointment makes you more optimistic but it is true. You see, a lot of people have the tendency to expect the worst out of a situation, as opposed to the best. They do this in an attempt to protect themselves from possible disappointment and to "not get their hopes up." This, however, keeps you from putting out the positive energy you need to receive the best. It is true that it is inevitable that you'll be disappointed. There is no getting around that. Yet, always expecting disappointment is not the answer here, as it will not soften the blow that disappointment deals. What will do that is to accept that you're going to be disappointed at some point or another in your life, while expecting the best. That way, you can enjoy the joyful feeling that comes with expecting the best, while armoring against disappointment (Shain, 2020).

Beyond these strategies, all the techniques that have thus far been covered throughout the course of *The Optimism Mindset Bible*, from visualization to affirmations and more, will undeniably help you to adopt a more positive mindset. You can always do a couple of additional, more minor things to further support your efforts in this matter, of course (Birt, 2022). For instance, you can:

- limit how much time you spend watching the news, because the news these tend to be really negative and you want to surround yourself with as much positivity as you can

- do more activities that you enjoy and that prove uplifting for you, as this will give you a much needed serotonin boost and lower your stress levels

- give yourself positive feedback, thereby increasing your internal motivation levels

- Engage in mindfulness practices such as meditation, which would be very useful in making your more self-aware

- learn to stop brushing compliments off and accepting them instead

- create self-care routines that work for you and that make you feel valued and cared for

- try new things whenever possible, since this is something optimistic people often do and since you might discover a brand new hobby or make some wonderful new memories in the process

Chapter 9:

Hypnosis

You can use hypnosis not as a cure but as a means of establishing a favorable climate in which to learn. –Milton H. Erickson

Hypnosis can be described as a deep state of focus and relaxation coupled with elevated levels of suggestibility (Sutton, 2021). The origins of hypnosis can be traced back to the 18th century, when a German physician called Franz Mesmer developed something called mesmerism. Mesmerism stated that human beings had a kind of animal magnetism that flowed through their body and affected their health. This flow had to be smooth and unhindered. Blockages to the flow were problematic because they could lead to both physical and emotional health problems.

Having come up with this idea, Mesmer started treating various patients using mesmerism and taught the technique to a variety of students. His treatments rapidly caught on in Paris and even drew the attention of King Louis XVI. The king commissioned a team of scientists to investigate mesmerism to prove whether it actually worked or not. Sadly, scientists eventually disproved mesmerism or at the very least the idea of having animal magnetism (Kotera, 2018). They found that this idea did not really have a scientific basis. Yet, just because animal magnetism couldn't be proven in the strictest sense, during the 18th century did not mean all of mesmerism was wrong. Especially since, the practice did seem to be curing a number of diseases or at the very least, their symptoms.

It would take a little while for mesmerism to become known as hypnotism and it would be a man called James Braid, not Franz Mesmer who coined that term. Braid was a Scottish ophthalmologist and clinician who actively followed Mesmer's work. The word he came up with for the practice—hypnosis—is a derivative of the Greek word for "sleep". Despite this, hypnotism does not actually have anything to do with sleep as modern scientists would later go on to prove. The two do have one key thing in common though and it is that both enhance your ability to focus but more on that later. To continue with hypnosis' rather fascinating history, the practice fell a bit out of vogue, until about the mid-19th century. It was then that an Austrian physician named Josef Breuer started using hypnosis to treat a patient's hysteria. He was able to use hypnosis to trigger the childhood emotions of this patient, whom he dubbed Anna O to protect her privacy, during sessions. As a result of this treatment there was a significant drop in Anna O's hysteric symptoms.

Breuer's work with Anna O and hypnosis caught the attention of another well-known psychologist: a man named Sigmund Freud. Perhaps you've heard of him? It was through hypnosis that Freud was able to discover the unconscious process, which then led to various significant findings in the field of psychoanalysis. Freud's work with hypnosis was carried even farther in the 20th century by a woman called Melanie Kline. Kline was one of the scientists who developed the object relations theory. Through her work Kline was able to conclude that Freud was being a little too stringent in his hypnosis work and that this adversely affected the effectiveness of the practice. For hypnosis to work, Kline found, you could not be authoritative with it.

Years later Kline's work was expanded on by yet another scientist, this time a man called Milton Erickson. Erickson is arguably one of the most influential figures when it comes to hypnosis. This psychiatrist developed a unique, rather creative language that could be used to effectively communicate with someone's unconscious when they were under hypnosis. In these unique conversations that Erickson held, he focused not on identifying the root causes of the symptoms his patients were having as either psychiatrist working with hypnosis had done before him, but on getting them to release these symptoms. The idea here was that he could get patients to do this by having them drop their defensive actions and attitudes using hypnosis. While a lot of people were skeptical of Erickson's approach the results ultimately spoke for themselves. Erickson's approach proved so successful that it was dubbed Ericksonian hypnosis and directly led to the development of neuro-linguistic programming (NLP).

Neuro-linguistic programming (NLP) is a technique that is used to alter people's thoughts, mindset, and behaviors. The idea here is that by using this technique you can help achieve whatever outcome you desire, be it manifesting success, overcoming a specific challenge, or something else entirely (Kandola, 2017). NLP is a unique hypnosis technique in that it brings together various communication, perceptual, and behavioral devices to accomplish its means. It was developed by John Grinder and Richard Bandler. The NLP process is pretty simple. You basically work to identify negative thought and behavioral patterns to change them. You also identify the thought and behavioral patterns of individuals you consider "successful" and then try to replace your own patterns with those.

Meanwhile, there was another surgeon in the 19th century that developed an interest in hypnotism. This British surgeon was called James Esdaile (1808-1859) and it was he who discovered that hypnotism could be used as a pain management method. Esdaile found hypnotism to be so effective in this regard that he started using it instead of anesthesia and in fact performed hundreds of operations that way. He did this in India, though, and while his findings were promising, British medical professionals were unwilling to listen to what he had to say when he came back to the United Kingdom. They much preferred sticking with anesthesia, it seemed, which was a decision that no doubt was influenced by the pharmaceutical powers that were in those years and that continues to affect our lives today whenever one of us has to go in for an operation these days (McKenna, 2015).

It was during this time that hypnotism became known as a part of alternative medicine. However, people's interest in hypnotism grew beyond that. Take French pharmacist Emile Coué, for instance. Another man of the 19th century, Coué met a medical professional who had made hypnosis a big part of his practice called Ambroise-Auguste Liébault. After working in Liébault's hypnosis clinic for two years, Coué developed a hypnotic induction technique called conscious autosuggestion (Robertson, 2009). Conscious autosuggestion was a method where the individual undergoing hypnosis was taught how to use suggestion and imagination to program their minds, so to speak. If you think that sounds like the meeting point of hypnosis and visualization, you're correct.

As you might have guessed from the name in conscious autosuggestion the person undergoing hypnosis remains conscious. In other words, they are neither in a trance nor asleep. Instead, they voluntarily accept the suggestions that are being made to them. Autosuggestion is based on two concepts. The first is that all suggestions can be considered autosuggestion. The second is that people experience internal conflict when their will and imagination struggle against one another. Generally speaking, though, their imagination ends up being stronger. As for the laws of autosuggestion, there are four, these being

- the law of concentrated attention
- the law of auxiliary emotion
- the law of reversed effort
- the law of subconscious teleology

The law of concentrated attention states that whatever you focus your attention on will come to pass. Sounds a lot like manifestation, doesn't it? The law of auxiliary emotion, meanwhile, dictates that if you feel very strong emotions about an idea, then you'll probably realize that idea suggestively. Again, sounds familiar. The law of reversed effort says that the more you try to consciously struggle against an obstacle, the bigger you make that obstacle, whereas the law of subconscious teleology affirms that whatever you suggest to your subconscious will always come to pass.

Judging by all this, it can be argued that Coué's personal brand of hypnosis is a form of manifestation and a very effective positive psychology tool. This becomes infinitely clearer when you take a look at how the method unfolds. If you want to practice conscious autosuggestion, you have to repeat the phrase or affirmation "Every day, in every way, I am getting better and better" to yourself 20 times a night. This works best when you whisper the words to yourself with your eyes closed. You can repeat the affirmation more than 20 times if you want but you shouldn't go too overboard. As you're repeating these words, you should place specific emphasis on the words "in every way" since that will function as a "catch all" suggestion.

Another way you can practice conscious autosuggestion is to simply repeat the phrase "It is going" or "It goes" about 20 times. This suggestion, while very simple, can help with pain management, especially if you repeat it while gently rubbing the part of your body that is in pain. If you have a headache, for instance, this might mean whispering those words to yourself with your eyes closed, and while rubbing your temples or forehead. As you can see from that example, Coué's method was partly about self-healing. In fact, he was a big believer of self-healing, to the point that he claimed that there was no such thing as hypnosis, only self-hypnosis (McKenna, 2015).

Today, hypnosis is a frequently used practice and this is thanks to many different scientists putting in the time and effort to prove that it works. Aside from the names we have already mentioned, there was Joseph Jastrow who began teaching hypnosis at the University of Wisconsin in the 20th century, thereby making it into a subject of academic interest. There was his student Clarke Hull, an experimental psychologist at Yale, who published the first major review written on hypnosis, applying it to modern psychology in the process, entitled *Hypnosis and Suggestibility*. There was also Andre Weitzenhoffer and Ernest Hilgard who began studying hypnosis at Stanford University, as well as the medical professionals who turned to the practice in the midst of WWI, WWII, and the Korean War to treat both various injuries and patients' trauma. It was through all these individuals' works that people ultimately began to recognize how hypnosis really worked, why it did, and what its myriad benefits were (Mongiovi, n.d.).

How Hypnotherapy Works

Hypnosis is a practice that you can do at home with some sort of guided app or program. However, if you've never done hypnosis before, working with a healthcare professional one-on-one is a good idea. That way, the guide you're working with can walk you through the process, step-by-step and review your treatment goals with you (Mayo Clinic Staff, 2022). Once that is done, your guide will usually kick things off by talking to you in a gentle, calm tone of voice. As they talk, they will describe scenes and images that make you feel safe, calm, and at peace.

After you've calmed down enough and entered into the kind of mindset you need to be in, your guide will start suggesting ways for you to achieve the goals you're chasing after. Let's say that you're a chain smoker and you're trying to manifest health. Therefore, you want to quit smoking. In this instance, your guide could suggest ways in which you could do this. Alternatively, they could bring visualization into the process and have you visualize a version of you where you're as healthy as you can be and a non-smoker at that.

It is important that you start your hypnosis journey with a guide because bringing yourself out of a hypnotic state can be a little challenging. You may or may not be able to do it by yourself and if you can't, then that is perfectly alright. That is part of the reason why your guide is there and it is their job to gently and gradually move you out of your relaxed state into a more and more alert one. It should be stated that being in a relaxed state while under hypnosis does not mean that you'll not remember what you said or that happened when you're brought out of it. You also will not lose control of your actions when you are under hypnosis, despite what Hollywood movies might have led you to believe.

Now, there are a variety of biological and psychological reasons as to why hypnosis works. When you undergo hypnosis, you enter into a highly relaxed state known as the "flow state" (Cummins, 2022). The reason you're able to enter into the flow state is that hypnosis quiets down the part of your brain that helps you to switch between different kinds of tasks. This region of your brain is disconnected from the part of it that directs your daydreaming and self-reflection abilities. So, when it is turned off, that part of your brain is able to become more active, hence the flow state. Additionally, studies show that when a person undergoes hypnosis, the area of their brain in charge of controlling autonomic bodily functions such as the beating of their heart or their breathing settles down as well (Fernandez et al., 2021). As a result, these processes slow down, making you much calmer.

The great thing about hypnosis is that while you should start with an in-person guide, you can eventually switch to solo practice sessions. In your sessions, you'll be able to reach that initial stage of calm and relaxation all by yourself, without getting any kind of help. You can turn to hypnosis apps or various videos on YouTube if you find that you need some help, though. The question then is, why would you want to? Yes, hypnosis can help treat the different symptoms of different conditions, as you've seen earlier. But are there any other benefits to it?

Benefits of Hypnosis

Hypnosis and, by extension, hypnotherapy have a legion of benefits to offer you. The most obvious of those benefits is that it does away with stress and anxiety and helps you manage these conditions (*Hypnosis: What It Is, Why It is Done, Benefits & Risks*, 2022). After all, you have to enter into a relaxed state of mind to be able to practice it. There are other mental health conditions that it can help treat too. For example, hypnosis was found to be a great treatment method for post-traumatic stress disorder (PTSD), as well as for phobias and panic attacks. At the same time, hypnosis could help you fix any behavioral issues you may have. Smoking, for example, is a behavioral issue you might want to change, given how badly it affects your health. Other behavioral issues the practice can help with include things like bedwetting and losing weight, especially if you're struggling with self-control or even things like binge eating.

Hypnosis is used to treat certain physical conditions, right alongside behavioral and mental health related ones. The annoying hot flashes you've during menopause can be made to go away with hypnosis and asthma can be managed with it. It can be the answer to any gastrointestinal disorders you're struggling with, including irritable bowel syndrome (IBS). Similarly, it can be a great pain management technique. This is why many doctors recommend hypnosis as a viable alternative to pain management medication in childbirth, as well as when dealing with migraines, headaches, burns, and even fibromyalgia and cancer.

On top of that, hypnosis is known to aid your efforts to deal with skin conditions such as psoriasis and warts and any unpleasant side effects that might come with radiation therapy, such as nausea. One of the most important benefits of the practice, though, is that it can help you to develop a positive mindset, considering how good having such a mindset is for you. Hypnosis can achieve this by helping you to unlearn any limiting beliefs you may have and negative thoughts you might be holding on to (Hoare, 2021). For this to work, you'd have to use hypnosis specifically for cultivating a positive mindset. The suggestions you receive while under hypnosis would have to focus on unlearning negative things and learning the positive messages you want to hold onto instead. Doing this can not only help you to cultivate a positive mindset, but also to adopt and hold onto positive habits, so long as you use hypnosis on a regular basis.

Like meditation and many of the other practices we have seen throughout this book, hypnosis works to the best effect if you do it every day. Just a 10 minute long hypnosis or self-hypnosis session can work wonders in your life. Repeating a couple of affirmations at the start of your practice is a good idea as it can make slipping into the relaxed state you need far easier to do. It can ward you against those negative thoughts and doubts that might try to creep into your mind otherwise. Over time, achieving that relaxed state and really absorbing the suggestions and messages you're giving yourself with hypnosis will become easier and easier, until one day you'll blink, surprised at just how much and how positively your life has changed in such a short span of time.

Given the relaxed state that hypnosis induces, it shouldn't be too surprising to hear that it can help you eliminate sleep issues such as insomnia and sleep walking (*6 Surprising Health Benefits of Hypnosis*, 2019). With insomnia, this connection is obvious. Hypnosis gets you to relax and let go of the stress that is likely keeping you up, thereby allowing you to drift off. With sleepwalking, the connection may be a little less obvious but it makes sense when you think about it. You can use the suggestions that hypnosis gives you, you see, to wake up when you get to your feet as you're sleepwalking. This can put an end to the habit pretty quickly, as you might imagine. In addition to this, self-hypnosis practices can increase the duration of your sleep while improving its quality.

Another fascinating connection can be found between hypnosis and weight loss. Studies show hypnosis sessions can help you to lose something like six pounds over the course of 18 months. Of course, this works best when you couple your hypnosis sessions with a healthy diet plan of some sort and an exercise schedule. The reason hypnosis can help with weight loss is that it trains your attention so that you become more likely to respond to any behavioral changes related to weight loss that'll be given to you as suggestions. These can actually make sticking with your exercise regimen and meal plans far easier to do.

Hypnosis Method 1: Conscious Breathing

A lot of people consider conscious breathing to be a mindfulness practice but it is actually a hypnotic one too. A regular adult draws in about 12 to 20 breaths per minute when they're not doing anything strenuous. They breathe without being conscious of it, primarily because we need to breathe to live. Conscious breathing actively draws your attention to your breathing. It makes you truly focus on it and in the process helps you to achieve a genuine state of calm. This, in turn, enables you to process negative thoughts, emotions, and even experiences better. Conscious breathing is often used in yoga and pranayama and it has many benefits to offer you (Hoshaw, 2022) including:

- a better quality of sleep
- lower blood pressure
- an elevated mood
- faster digestion and metabolism
- better cardiovascular health

Most importantly though, it helps you to manage your stress and anxiety better, keeping them from poisoning your mindset. There are a great many types of conscious breathing techniques to choose from and all of them can offer you these benefits. As a newcomer, though, the ones that you can opt for are diaphragmatic breathing, box breathing, and Kapalabhati, otherwise known as breath of fire.

Diaphragmatic breathing is a type of deep breathing that can have an instant calming effect on you. To start, you have to either sit or lie down on your back somewhere comfortable. Place one hand on your chest and the other right below your rib cage, which'll be above the muscle known as the diaphragm. Now, relax your shoulders so that they're not pulled up toward your ears. Turn your attention to your breathing and take a deep breath in through your nose and keep going until you can't any further. As you breathe in, focus on directing all that air flow to your diaphragm. You should feel the hand over your diaphragm rise up. You should also feel how tight your skin becomes as you breathe in. You should be doing all this pretty slowly. Meanwhile, you should not feel the hand on your chest rise up at all. Once your diaphragm is fully expanded, purse your lips and slowly let all that air out, feeling the hand on your diaphragm fall back down and feeling your stomach gently contact. This should last about four seconds. Once you've expelled all that air, draw in another breath and keep going like that. Slowly, breathe in and out, keeping your attention on your breath and how it feels as it travels through your nostrils and airways and fills your diaphragm. Try to breathe in and out like this between six to ten times. After a couple of breaths, you'll notice you've become remarkably calmer (Jewell & Hoshaw, 2018).

Alternatively, you can try box breathing, which can both help you with stress and anxiety management by ushering you into a calm state, and significantly improve your concentration and performance levels (Gotter, 2017). Box breathing is such an effective conscious breathing method that individuals in high stress jobs, like Navy SEALS and police officers, often use it. To begin, you have to sit down somewhere comfortable or lie down on your back. Place your hands on your lap but turn your palms to face the sky. Direct your attention to your posture so that you're sitting up straight and thus, able to breathe in deeply. Now, slowly exhale through your mouth, trying to expel all the air from your lungs. This should take around four seconds. Then, slowly inhale through your nose, slowly counting to four as you go. Pay attention to your lungs fully. Feel each and every section of your lungs expand and fill up and then take note of how the air moves down to your abdomen. When your lungs are fully inflated, hold your breath for four seconds, then slowly exhale again, counting to four as you go. Hold your breath for another four seconds, before you inhale once more. Keep going like this for four cycles at least, more if you need to. Stop immediately if you get dizzy and give yourself a full minute before trying again.

The final conscious breathing technique you can try is breath of fire, which is a form of pranayama or breath control. To practice this technique, you have to be sitting down and can't lie down. Your session can last anywhere from 30 seconds to 10 minutes and how long it lasts will depend on you (Nunez, 2020). By practicing breath of fire, you'll not only relieve your stress and anxiety, but also improve your concentration, mindfulness, respiratory abilities, and even digestion. You can start practicing the technique by sitting down cross legged and keeping your back straight. You can put your hands either on your knees with your palms facing up or you can keep one hand there while putting the other on your stomach.

Once you are in position, take a deep, slow breath through your nose and feel your belly expand as you do so. Then forcefully expel all that air through your nose without pausing. You should feel both your abdominal muscles and your nostrils contract at this. Despite this obvious difference in how you breathe in and out, the duration of your inhalations and exhalations should be the same. After you've established a rhythm, keep going until you grow comfortable with it. Then speed things up so that your exhalations become loud and powerful. Keep going in this manner for at least 30 seconds, longer if you'd like.

Hypnosis Method 2: Guided Visualization

You already know that visualization is a powerful mental tool, but did you know it can be a very good hypnosis practice too? This is true for some types of guided visualizations at least, like color breathing. Color breathing is a great exercise for managing stress and improving your general mood. It also makes for a rather vivid and entertaining session. You start by getting into a comfortable, seated position, though you can lie down if you'd like. Then, you close your eyes and start breathing deeply, the way you'd with any conscious breathing exercise. At this point you choose a color, let's say it is sky blue, and visualize it. You keep breathing in and out while holding that color in your mind's eye, describing what it means and represents for you in your thoughts. As you inhale, you visualize sky blue filtering in through your nostrils, traveling down your airways, filling up your lungs, and then dispersing to each and every corner of your body, from the crown of your head to the tips of your toes. As you exhale, you visualize any unwanted feelings, thoughts, and sensations being expelled from your body along with your breath. You keep going like this for however long you'd like or until your session is over.

Since color breathing is a guided visualization practice, the person you're with or the app that you are using will give you specific instructions as you go along. They will similarly do this with another visualization practice called progressive muscle relaxation. This, as you can tell from the name, is an immensely helpful exercise for anxiety and stress. It works wonders for emotional tension and improving the quality of your sleep too. The first step in your progressive muscle relaxation practice will be to lie on your back somewhere comfortable. Once you're settled, you can close your eyes and focus on just your breathing for a little bit. When you're ready, you start tensing and relaxing the various muscle groups throughout your body, starting with the ones that aren't bothering you at the moment. You do this for every muscle group, even the ones in your toes and feet.

One thing that'll make the practice easier for you is to either start from the bottom and work your way up or to do the exact opposite. What you want to do as you tense your muscles is to inhale deeply and slowly, hold that breath and the tension for five seconds, and then gently let both go. As you do, you should envision the tension you felt in your muscles draining out of your body, the way tension would leave a coiled spring. You should put about 10 seconds of rest time between the different muscle groups as you work your way through them and keep going until you've tended to them all.

One of the most effective guided visualization techniques you can ever try is called guided imagery. Guided imagery takes the "happy place" approach we have discussed in earlier chapters to a whole new level and allows you to achieve a true sense of peace. To start, you have to either lie down or sit in a comfortable position, then calm your breathing down with some conscious breathing exercises. That done, you can start visualizing somewhere that you genuinely find calm and peaceful. This could be somewhere you know, like your childhood bedroom, or somewhere you'd like to be like a beautiful beach or a lush green meadow. As you visualize this place, your guide or guided app will direct your attention to the sensory details you can notice about it. How warm is it where you are? What scents can you smell and sounds can you hear? What does it feel like to be in this space? The deeper you get into these details, the more vivid and real that place will become for you and the deeper the level of calm you achieve will be. This effect will only be compounded as you imagine peace and calm entering into your lungs and very veins with each breath.

Hypnosis Method 3: Positive Suggestions

Positive suggestions are a hypnosis practice that's built on positive affirmations. To start, you'll of course have to choose or write some good affirmations for yourself. It's a great way of overcoming limiting beliefs using the power of the relaxed state that hypnosis puts you in and affirmations' own ability to help you for new beliefs, especially when they are about you. This practice can therefore both alter your subconscious in some very significant ways and help you to create more positive thinking patterns.

Once you've chosen your affirmation you can kickstart this whole process by finding a calm, relaxing environment and taking a seat or lying down on your back. You can then close your eyes and take a couple of deep breaths. When you're ready, meaning when your heart and breathing rates have settled down, you can turn your attention to your chosen affirmation. What you want to do here is to repeat that affirmation to yourself, slowly and out loud. As you do so, you want to really focus your mind on what it means for you and try to feel it resonate within your very bones. This may take a couple of repetitions and saying your affirmation—"I am worthy of love," for instance—with conviction should help. As you keep repeating that phrase, you should try to tune into the positive feelings it generates. It doesn't matter if you can name those feelings for now. That won't make them any less real or significant and you'll be able to label them more easily as time goes on. For the time being, you can focus solely on the sensations that they generate and where in your body you can feel them.

By steadily engaging in this practice every day or at least every couple of days, for about a minute or so, you can slowly build a positive, calm, and nourishing mentality for yourself. You can create the kind of mental atmosphere that is truly conducive to change and come to believe and embody all the positive thoughts you create.

Hypnosis Method 4: Regressive Counting

You've probably heard of this method before because hypnosis is often associated with counting. You hear the word "hypnosis" and you expect it to be followed by the words, "1,2,3, and sleep!" While this mostly isn't the case, regressive counting is a hypnosis technique that has you make use of the power of numbers. In doing so, it enables you to achieve a state of deep relaxation and consciousness. The method itself is fairly simple, which is why it is often used in self-hypnosis, which we'll get to in a moment. One of the most important benefits of regressive counting is that it can improve your focus and memory greatly. Another is that practicing it regularly—a couple of times a week—can help you to reach a state of inner calm that will last you for a long time to come.

If you want to practice regressive counting, you have to first either lie down on your back or sit and get comfortable. Ideally, you want to be somewhere quiet and calm, where you won't be interrupted while you do this. As usual, you start by taking some deep, calming breaths. When you're ready, you choose a high number—say 100—and you slowly start counting down. You can do this mentally, while whispering to yourself, or fully out loud if you'd like. As you count down, you imagine that each and every number that you hit brings you closer and closer to calm and relaxation. That's why you count down, as opposed to counting up.

Now, as with in meditation, your mind might occasionally wander off during your regressive counting exercise and dive down different avenues of thought. While this is to be expected and thus not something you should chastise yourself over, you should gently bring your attention back to your counting every time it happens. Mind you, this might happen several times if you're a beginner at regressive counting, especially if you've chosen a very high number. As such, it is vital that you be patient with yourself as you keep going. Over time, you'll find that staying on task gets easier and easier to do and before you know it, you'll be able to turn to regressive counting whenever you'd like. As a result, you'll be able enter into the relaxed, alert state of mind you'd like to be in without any delays or issues.

Hypnosis Method 5: Relaxation Anchors

Relaxation anchors or anchoring is a hypnosis technique that uses a specific gesture or signal that gets you to enter into a relaxed state of mind. That Hollywood version of hypnosis where a magician says "When I snap my fingers you'll start acting like a chicken," is a version of this, though an exaggerated and highly inaccurate one. The reason anchoring—real anchoring—works is that it gets your mind to form a connection between the gesture you've chosen as an anchor, like rubbing the skin between your thumb and forefinger for instance, and the relaxed state you're looking for. Once a mental bridge forms between the two, you become able to drop into a calm and peaceful state simply by crossing it.

For anchoring to work, you need to first choose an anchor that works for you. This might be an object that you carry around with you and that you can look at or touch whenever you need to calm down. It might be a gesture too or a phrase or word that you utter to yourself. Whatever your anchor is, it is vital that you make it something easy to recall and turn to whenever you need to. If you're panicking and can't remember what your anchor was because you chose something overly complicated because it sounded cool, then that's going to be a problem for you.

Choosing your anchor is just step one of the process. Step two is sitting or lying down somewhere calm and in a comfortable position. That done, you need to first calm down a bit and practice like conscious breathing or progressive relaxation can help you with that. After you've sufficiently relaxed, you can bring your anchor into the picture. For example, if your anchor really is rubbing that patch of skin between your thumb and forefinger, you can do that now. This way, you'll strengthen the bridge between the calm you're experiencing and the physical sensation you're giving yourself. The more you do this, the stronger that bridge will become, of course. Practice regularly and after a certain point, just touching that patch of skin will be enough to get you to relax. Thus, that anchor will firmly take root and you'll be able to make use of it whenever you feel stressed, anxious, or anything of the sort.

Hypnosis Method 6: Guided Self-Hypnosis

A final hypnosis method you can try is guided self-hypnosis. You can try guided self-hypnosis using apps or recordings that are specifically designed to induce a hypnotic state. They can be very useful and while it may take a little bit of time to get into them, once you do, it won't take you long to see the immense benefits they have to offer you. To start, you'll have to find either an app or recording you like. While YouTube is chock full of these you may want to do just a little bit of research online, so that you can be sure you are using a trusted source.

After you've found the source that's just right for you, you can choose a guided self-hypnosis session that is in line with what you're looking for. Then you can sit or lie down in a comfortable position, somewhere calm and quiet. If you're somewhere a bit noisier than you'd like, you can put in your headphones to better concentrate. What will happen next is that the recording you've chosen will walk you through a series of visualizations and positive suggestions. These will reinforce the messages you're trying to give your subconscious mind and over time, allow it to soak them in. In the process, it'll make it possible for your mind to assimilate the messages it is receiving. Not only will guided self-hypnosis sessions get you into a highly relaxed state of mind, but they'll also open up your mind to greater possibilities, make you feel more connected to yourself reduce your stress and anxiety levels, and even improve your self-confidence, thereby helping you to make some very positive changes in your life.

Hypnosis and Positive Psychology

Generally speaking, hypnosis and hypnotherapy are great tools to consider when you're trying to manifest the things you want. One of the key rules to remember in positive psychology and manifestation for that matter is that you'll inevitably end up amplifying whatever you focus on (Yapko, n.d.). Hypnosis is a great way of training your attention on the things that you really want, be that health, love, changing a problematic behavior like smoking, or something else entirely. At the same time, hypnosis can draw your attention to any skills and abilities that you have that you're either undervaluing or unaware of. In this sense, hypnosis can provide people with a comprehensive, whole view of themselves.

In a similar way, hypnosis can be used to generate and focus more on positive thoughts. This can be done through both suggestion and self-suggestion. It can make doing things like practicing positive self-talk easier and enable you to shift from a pessimistic and fixed mindset to an optimistic and growth-oriented one (Anbar, 2021). By allowing you to tap into your subconscious mind, hypnosis can grant you access to wisdom and knowledge that you, again, did not realize you had. This can, in turn, drive you to explore these things even more, further strengthening your growth mindset.

Throughout this chapter, you've explored a variety of simple self-hypnosis techniques that you can practice whenever and wherever you'd like. These methods can make for powerful ways of entering a state of trance and influencing your subconscious mind in positive ways. Guided visualizations, for example, can help you create vivid, realistic images of your desired goals. Progressive relaxation and conscious breathing techniques can make you relax and let go of no small amount of stress and tension. Regressive counting can do the same while improving your focus, anchoring can make entering into relaxed states of being easier, and self-hypnosis can enable you to achieve the positive mindset you truly want.

Of these methods, though, it is self-hypnosis that can really boost your ability to use the power of your subconscious mind to create positive changes in your life. This will take some time and dedication on your part, though, and it is to be expected that you get immediate results. That's alright. It's over time that you'll develop a deeper connection with your subconscious and achieve the kind of transformative experience that positive psychology is all about. One of the prime reasons why hypnosis is a tool and part of positive psychology is that it is a flow exercise. "Flow" is something the scientist Mihaly Csikszentmihalyi has been actively researching since the 1970s (*Positive Psychology - Key Theories and Applications to Hypnotherapy*, n.d.). Flow, as you know, is a human experience where you become completely absorbed in whatever you're doing. Losing track of time while painting, for example, is a flow experience. So is hypnosis. You can tell that you're having a flow experience when you've achieved a kind of balance between a challenge that is being presented to you and your faith in your ability to meet and overcome that challenge. The bigger the challenge you're presented with, the greater your ability to meet it will be, and the more you'll become absorbed in what you're doing.

Flow experiences are good for you because they generate a lot of positive emotions. This makes you even more engaged in your work, which in turn improves your performance. Understandably, this results in you enjoying your work more, which leads to more positive emotions and so, you become caught in a loop—a good one, for a change. Since hypnosis is a flow experience, all these stages apply to it. This is especially true for sessions where hypnosis is used to focus someone's attention on other flow experiences and the strengths that are to be found in them. It is also true for sessions where hypnosis is used to train an individual to enter into a flow state in their everyday life, since that can help them manage stress better and generate more positive emotions throughout their day. In this regard, hypnosis and hypnotherapy can be as effective as any positive psychology practice, such as affirmations. Affirmations, as you've seen, can even be made part of some hypnosis practices and sessions. By now, you know why affirmations really work and what you need to do to write the perfect ones. Why do affirmations really work in the first place though? What is it about them that makes them so effective on a neurological and psychological level? Let's find out!

Chapter 10:

Affirmations

It is the repetition of affirmations that lead to belief. And once that belief becomes a deep conviction, things begin to happen. –Muhammad Ali

By now, you're well acquainted with the many benefits that affirmations have to offer you. You might, however, be slightly confused as to why they work. Yes, affirmations get your mind to believe in something, since it can't really distinguish between what's real and what's not, and in the process, make what you believe into your actual reality. How exactly does that happen? Why does it happen? Is that the only reason affirmations work? Where do affirmations really come from, anyways?

To start with that last question, affirmations have been around for thousands of years. Originally, they were called mantras and were invented by Buddhists and Hindus as a way to quiet the mind. The idea here was that mantras could help people to achieve a calm state of being and focus on higher truths instead. Some people still refer to affirmations as mantras but it wasn't until the 17th century that the word "affirmation" was used for the first time. The first person to use it in recorded history was a philosopher called Reneé Descartes (*Who Invented Affirmations? A Brief History of Positive Self-Talk*, n.d.). Perhaps you've heard of him? Descartes is best known for his saying "I think therefore I am". However, the root of the modern day iteration of affirmations goes back to the 19th century United States. This was when a spiritual movement called the New Thought Movement came onto the scene.

The movement was essentially a conglomeration of different beliefs and practices, including things like positive self-talk and affirmations. At the time, the New Thought Movement took the country by storm. These days, the movement is not all that big, at least compared to other belief systems. Yet the various practices they helped to spread can still be found all around us. Obviously, this includes affirmations. To date, many studies have been conducted proving that affirmations work and showing why they work in the first place. There's also been a staggering amount of success stories, some of which appear hard to believe. Take Louise Hay, for example. Louise Hay is a pioneer in the field of health affirmations. She strongly believes that affirmations can be used for self-healing and given the things that she went through, this belief is not exactly groundless. Hay was diagnosed with cervical cancer, you see, and her odds of survival weren't great to put it very mildly. Despite this, Hay refused traditional medical treatment because they ran counter to her beliefs.

You would think that a woman diagnosed with cervical cancer wouldn't be able to live for much longer without treatment. You'd be wrong. Upon receiving her diagnosis Hay turned to some self-reflection to figure out why this might have happened. She reasoned that her past experiences, which included rape, teenage pregnancy, and physical abuse, led to her illness. This was in keeping with her belief that negative experiences that result in emotional and physical turmoil lead to a variety of different illnesses. Using that as a basis, Hay self-healing techniques. Affirmations were featured pretty heavily among them and they worked. Hay not only beat cancer without treatment, but she went on to become a major author and publisher, a profession she still enjoys at 80 years old (*How Successful People Have Used Positive Affirmations throughout History*, n.d.).

Another champion of healing affirmations is Dr. Bernie Siegel who often worked with terminally ill patients. Dr. Siegel was the kind of surgeon that liked a personal touch and so grew close with many of his patients, going on to learn their life stories. After a while, he noticed that a common theme was emerging where a lot of his patients had experienced trauma of some kind in their lives. Dr. Siegel thus developed this theory that healing that trauma could go a long way to healing his patients' physical ailments. So, he tried doing what he could. He became a sort of surrogate father for his patients, no matter what their age, providing them with ample support and love. He had them regularly practice healing affirmations, as well as do creative visualization exercises and therapeutic drawings. The program worked incredibly well. Patients not only recovered from their illnesses much more quickly, but some were able to bounce back from diseases and conditions that should have been far too progressed for that.

These are just some real life examples demonstrating how effective positive affirmations can be. It must be stressed, however, that the take away from them is not skipping traditional medical help if you need it.

What you want to do instead is get the aid you want and couple it with positive affirmations. What you want to do is take aligned action with the thing you're trying to get and manifest, be it health, wealth, love, or something else. Having said that, the question still remains: Why exactly do affirmations work? To understand this, we are going to have to take a closer look at our brains to see how affirmations affect them.

Your Brain on Affirmations

Positive affirmations affect you on a neurological level. In other words, they affect your very brain. A study was conducted a few years ago to uncover whether this really was the case or not. This study involves taking MRI scans of people's brains as they repeated their chosen positive affirmations to themselves. The scans showed that the reward centers of people's brains quite literally lit up as they recited their affirmations, in the same way that eating a piece of chocolate cake or winning a bike race would (Dutcher et al., 2016). This means that every time you repeat an affirmation to themself, the neural pathways in the part of your brain that's able to make you feel happy and positive become active.

This makes a great deal of sense when you consider how using positive affirmations on a daily basis can make you feel good and put you in a more positive, optimistic frame of mind. It also explains why positive affirmations can help you with stress management. When the pleasure center of your brain turns on, hormones like serotonin which make you feel good flood your system. These counter the effects of stress hormones like cortisol and slow down, then halt their production. So, you start feeling a whole lot less stress and a lot more calm, without all that cortisol getting your heart to beat faster and your lungs to work overtime. This physiological effect is another thing that positive affirmations can achieve.

Interestingly enough, two additional parts of your brain that become active when you practice positive affirmations. These are the medial prefrontal cortex and posterior cingulate (Hampton, 2019). These regions of the brain are in charge of processing any information that you'd recognize as negative, painful, and threatening. If, for example, someone were to hurl accusations at you, these regions would be working to process them, thus enabling you to respond accordingly. What if someone were to just offer your constructive criticism, though? Well, if your prefrontal cortex and posterior cingulate weren't active, you won't be able to process that feedback. As a result, you'd be far more likely to take it as criticism, judgment, or even as accusations.

In other words, you'd be liable to mistake constructive feedback for a threat. In response, you'd likely get pretty defensive and maybe even aggressive since that is how most people deal with threats. This kind of behavior can be pretty hurtful, as you know, especially when the person giving you feedback only means to help. Since people are also likely to lash out when they are hurt, the person who is giving you feedback can get defensive as well. Pretty soon, you might find yourself in a full blown argument with someone you actually care about. This could significantly damage your relationship with them in both the short and long term. Positive affirmations can prevent all this from happening by activating your prefrontal cortex and posterior cingulate on a regular basis, thus giving you the ability to discern between helpful feedback, which is not a threat, and unfair criticism, which can be a threat.

The reason various parts of your brain become more active when you use positive affirmations is neuroplasticity. Now, you might remember neuroplasticity from our earlier discussions of affirmations. Neuroplasticity is your brain's ability to reconfigure itself. It's the method it used-s to dissolve connections, which are formed by your neurons, between the different parts of your brain (Kelly, 2014). When a neuron in your brain wants to say something to another neuron, it will send an electrochemical signal. This signal will travel down a sort of thread, known as an axon, that connects those two neurons. If the threat in question is the highway between the neurons, then the signal itself is the passenger, which means that it needs a car. That car is something known as a neurotransmitter, a chemical that's tasked with getting signals from one neuron to the next.

When your neurons communicate with one another, sending signals to and from, the chemicals they are carried in cause certain other chemicals, like oxytocin to be created. These, in turn, trigger various hormones, like serotonin and cortisol, causing you to have some kind of emotional reaction to a situation that you're in or a thought that you're having. This is why negative thoughts have the power to make you feel bad while positive thoughts have the power to make you feel good, to put things very simply. The problem with this is that the more you think negative thoughts, the stronger and more those highways your neurotransmitters travel down become. When that happens you become even more likely to keep using those highways and thinking those thoughts. This problem, though, is also a solution because the same thing happens with positive thoughts. The more you think them, the stronger their highways, and the more positive your general thinking. This logic applies to positive affirmations too. The more you repeat them to yourself, the more defined their axons will become—which is neuroplasticity in effect—and the more often you'll use them. The more you use them the greater their effect will be on your mindset.

There is one other, very interesting connection between the human brain and affirmations and it is that all these different brain regions—the pleasure center, the medial prefrontal cortex, and the posterior cingulate, become more active when you use future-oriented affirmations as opposed to past-oriented ones (Cascio et al., 2015). This is why you need to use affirmations in the present tense and have them focus on the future. It's why such affirmations generate more positive emotions and make you more likely to take aligned action, while increasing your odds of success. All of this is why affirmations can significantly raise your sense of self-worth and self-esteem, coming to play a crucial role in your ability to understand your own identity in the process.

A Quick Note on Self-Identity Theory

Aside from being provable on a neurological level, positive affirmations are built on a very solid foundation known as self-identity theory. Self-identity theory that you are able to maintain a sense of self-integrity by telling yourself the things you believe in in a positive manner (Moore, 2019). Put another way, the theory's underpinning is that you can ensure your self-integrity through positive affirmations. Your self-integrity is your perceived ability to control various outcomes of the situations you are in and respond to perceived threats in a healthy way. Someone with a healthy sense of self-integrity, for example, is someone who can recognize the difference between helpful feedback and hurtful criticism and not mistake one for the other. Furthermore, it is someone that can respond to both in a healthy way and without letting either get them into a horrible mood for the rest of the day.

Self-integrity, then, is something that basically makes it possible for you to protect yourself from different threats. Hence, so is self-affirmation. Self-affirmation enables you to do this because it helps you weave and hold onto a narrative about yourself where you're a good, moral, and capable person that can adapt to a variety of different circumstances. It keeps you flexible and cultivates a growth and abundance mindset, as opposed to a fixed and scarcity mindset, the benefits of which you already know. At the same time, self-affirmation allows you to let go of the belief that you have to be perfect. Instead, it makes it possible for you to strive to be competent in things you're good at doing and that you enjoy doing. This, in turn, gives you the ability to engage in things that you actually find value in. On top of that, self-affirmation makes you more internally motivated, rather than being dependent on external sources of motivation like praise.

It is thanks to these three things that affirmations confirm your sense of self-integrity and feed into your sense of self-identity. How exactly do they do this on a psychological level then? To understand the answer to this question, we have to take a look at how affirmations affect your subconscious and make use of some shortcuts that it has created for itself.

Taking Advantage of Your Mind's Laziness

The thing about the human brain and mind is that, as useful and impressive as they are, they are kind of lazy. They like working smart as opposed to hard, though that they work hard when they have to is undeniable. To that end, they create certain shortcuts to make their jobs—of which there are many—easier and quicker to do (*The Science behind Positive Affirmations*, 2021). On the whole there are three such shortcuts, these being:

- the Dunning-Kruger Effect
- the Observational Selection Bias
- confirmation bias

To start with the Dunning-Kruger Effect this is a cognitive bias— meaning mental shortcut—where an individual would overestimate or underestimate their skills, thus being unable to see themselves clearly. The observational selection bias, on the other hand, is a person's tendency to notice something more once you've noticed it at least once. As for confirmation bias, this is a person's tendency to look for and believe more in things that confirm their existing beliefs. These three things are officially known as cognitive biases and, as mentioned, they're shortcuts that your brain and mind have developed to make decisions really quickly. Otherwise, they'd have to think everything through really carefully and thoroughly and that takes up a lot of time and energy. When you use a cognitive bias, however, you become able to make split second decisions and move through your day quickly, without having to go through too much agonizing. Naturally, these cognitive biases are all subconscious processes, meaning you don't even realize you're using them. This doesn't mean, however, that you can't hijack these processes. In fact, you can and regularly using positive affirmations will allow you to do so.

Affirmations can actually be considered cognitive biases. The main things that set them apart from other cognitive biases are that they are used intentionally and that they reinforce positive messages, not negative ones. Affirmations that declare how amazing you are at one kind of skill or another—writing, communicating, coding, etc.—are cognitive biases that use the Dunning-Kruger Effect to your advantage. Affirmations that focus on how much love there is in your life or how deserving you are of it use Observational Selection Bias to your advantage. After all, once you start repeating these to yourself, you kick this bias into action and start noticing all the loving things that the people in your life do for you. Furthermore, you become more aware of the positive sides of you, ones that you feel are "deserving" of love. To be clear, every part of you is deserving of this, but noticing your own positive qualities makes accepting this fact a lot easier to do. As for confirmation bias, affirmations use this in much the same way. Once you've established the belief you keep repeating to yourself—"I am deserving of love," let's say—you start actively, though not necessarily consciously, looking for evidence that proves as much.

As previously established, a big reason why cognitive biases and therefore affirmations work is that your subconscious mind cannot distinguish between what's real and what's not. This is because to your brain, whatever you imagine is a neurological reality that you're living through. Say that you have agoraphobia, which is a fear of spiders. You're sitting there in a park, harmlessly daydreaming. As your mind wanders here to there, you imagine a small or maybe not so small spider creeping up onto the bench you're sitting on. You see the image very clearly in your mind's eye: How the spider slowly makes its way up on the bench, walks toward you, and scrambles up your leg. Your leg jerks in real life trying to throw the thing off. Your eyes shoot open, your hand tries to brush the arachnid off your knee, only to find it isn't there. There's nothing there. You stare at your knee for a minute, startled, waiting for your furiously pounding heart to calm down, your rapid breathing to subside.

This, obviously, is an extreme example of how your brain can mistake the imaginary for reality but it is one that people with anxiety disorders like phobias experience often. One study, which was conducted with a group who actually had various phobias, found that when people imagined themselves confronting their fears the part of their brain that processes fear—the nucleus accumbens—became incredibly active. So did another part of the brain called the ventromedial prefrontal cortex, which is in charge of assessing and evading risks and threats (University of Colorado at Boulder, 2018). This kind of thing doesn't just happen with phobias nor does it only happen with "visualization" exercises, which is how we might define our spider exercise. It applies to anything and everything your mind creates, including negative thoughts, cognitive biases, positive affirmations, and beliefs. Once these things take hold, they in turn shape your reality, for good or bad.

A great example of how your beliefs can shape your reality can be seen in the placebo effect (Hamilton, 2019). The placebo effect is something that takes place when you're given what you're told is a drug that can take care of some ailment or other but that's really something wholly ineffective. Say that you have a headache and someone gives you a pill that they tell you is Advil. You swallow it down without hesitation. A little while later you find that your headache has subsided completely. In this instance, the pill you've taken has had no effect on your pain. Your brain's expectation and belief that it would, however, played a major part in it. That expectation caused your brain to start believing the pain was going away and so the pain went away. If your brain is able to do this with something as physical as a headache, imagine what it could do with the affirmations you write and repeat to yourself. Affirmations are the first steps you need to take to start believing in the things you want to make a reality. Once you've established your beliefs they are your very reality itself.

Affirmations and Beliefs

A belief is essentially an idea that you take as a statement of fact. It is something that you, as an individual, hold true, though others might not necessarily agree with you. Some of your beliefs serve you. They make you more motivated, energetic, enthusiastic, and happier overall. Some of your beliefs, like limiting beliefs, as you've seen, do the exact opposite of this. They demotivate you, hold you back, keep you from going after the things you want, and give up at the first sign of trouble. Your positive beliefs obviously do the former. Your negative beliefs, of which you sadly have plenty, do the latter. The good news is that positive affirmations can very easily turn into your new beliefs about yourself. For that to happen, however, you need to put in a little bit of work. If you're only repeating your affirmations to yourself every once in a while and not on a regular basis, then the odds of them altering your reality and turning into your new beliefs are low. How regularly you use your affirmations can play a crucial role in shaping your beliefs. That's not the only thing that can though. For example, one way you can turn affirmations into beliefs is to choose ones that are actually true for you now, to a certain degree (*How to Turn Affirmations into Beliefs*, 2018). As an example, say that you want to be in a genuinely loving, caring relationship. Writing an affirmation like "I am in a great relationship," might make you feel good but it won't be true, at least not yet. Writing

"I am deserving of love and welcome it into my life," on the other hand, is.

This kind of affirmation would be better able to impact your beliefs because it has to do with the underlying quality—love—that the relationship you want your relationship to provide you with. Before you write an affirmation for yourself, then, you should think carefully about what you believe the thing you want will truly provide you with. As another example, if you want to write an affirmation to manifest abundance, the qualities you may identify that are associated with it could be freedom, comfort, and joy. That being the case, you might consider using these specific words in your affirmations, thereby inviting them into your life.

Just as affirmations use your cognitive biases to your advantage, your cognitive biases can be used to strengthen your affirmations and help them turn into your beliefs. If you are using an affirmation about how worthy you are of love, for instance, then making a conscious effort to notice all the love in your life will work to your advantage. It will, at the very least, make you more mindful of all the people in your life that genuinely care about you, something that you might be prone to take for granted. This will make you feel more secure and grateful, as well as safer to seek healthy forms of love in your life. Furthermore, it will reaffirm the belief that you're trying to form through your affirmation, which is that you deserve the kind of love you want, since the evidence supporting it will already be at hand.

Aside from helping you to establish firm, positive beliefs affirmations can enable you to dismantle the negative beliefs you hold onto. This will take a little bit of time, as you know, but you can hasten the process. The first step you need to take to accomplish this is to make a list of all the negative qualities that you believe define you or apply to you (Alexander, 2011). This list should include everything you can think of from any chastisements you regularly offer yourself—like "I'm so stupid"—to any criticism your parents or siblings may have levied against you when you were a child, and to any negative feedback you received in your last performance review. You shouldn't let the qualities on this list affect you negatively as you're working on it. You also shouldn't judge yourself for these perceived flaws or imperfections. At the very least, you should try not to do so.

Once you are finished with your list, you should go over it with a critical eye to see if any can be grouped together under a common theme like "I am unworthy of love" or "I am incompetent." These will be the core, recurring beliefs that those negative thoughts are stemming from and it will be these things you'll be changing through your affirmations. Anytime you identify a recurring belief, you should write it down in your notebook. As you're writing it down, you should ask yourself where in your body you can feel it, specifically. You might be feeling it, for example, in your gut. You might alternatively be feeling it in your heart or notice that the belief is often accompanied by a slight headache. Making note of these sensations is important because this will help you become more aware of the times when you get caught by your negative recurrent beliefs without realizing it. Sometimes your mind works so fast, after all, that you don't realize you're thinking specific thoughts. In these cases, you can realize what sensations you're having in your body, though, and use them as signs that you're getting caught up in negative thinking patterns. Since you'll know which sensation is associated with which recurring thought, you'll be able to turn to its corresponding positive affirmation to put an end to things.

Before that, though, you'll need to write down what your affirmations are. Your affirmations will have to do with your core, recurrent, negative beliefs, as mentioned before. One way to do this is to write one that either focuses on the positive qualities that you possess that would actively counter the negative qualities you keep assigning yourself. Another is to find a positive side to a seemingly negative quality you have and write an affirmation around it. If you think that you're "lazy", for instance, one affirmation to write might be "I know when to work hard and when to stop taking care of my physical and mental well-being." You can write a shorter version of this too, since keeping affirmations on the shorter side is a good idea.

Once you've settled on your affirmations, you'll have to repeat them to yourself every day. Repetition is key to changing beliefs, as you know. One great strategy you can employ here is to speak your affirmations out loud to yourself three times a day, meaning morning, noon, and night, for up to five minutes. This would equal 15 minutes of repetition, which isn't all that long in the grand scheme of things. A day lasts 24 hours, after all, and even if you spend eight of those hours sleeping, you'll still have 16 to use however you'd like. Another strategy to use is to anchor the affirmations that you're repeating to your body by placing one hand on the region where you felt unpleasant sensations while you were having specific negative thoughts. That way, you'll be able to alter both the thought in question and the sensation you're feeling. What's more, you'll be able to breathe in the affirmation as you're repeating it and start to embody the quality that you're seeking.

Affirmations are mostly solo exercises but you can enlist the help of a trusted friend, family member, or even life coach or therapist when you're working to turn them into your new beliefs. If one of your affirmations is "I am cherished", then asking someone to tell you that "You're cherished" will support the belief you're forming. This technique is something that parents use for their kids a lot so that they can help them establish positive beliefs about themselves. As such, it is referred to as "good mothering" or "good fathering" by psychologists. What if you don't have someone you can ask to do this or what if you're not comfortable with the idea of doing this yet? If that's the case, you can practice your affirmations in front of a mirror, thereby getting your own reflection to reaffirm the positive messages you're giving yourself.

Following these steps can be highly effective in changing your core, recurring beliefs. Changing them is something you honestly owe yourself, given how your beliefs can impact your decision making and actions. The very interesting thing about beliefs is that you start a kind of chain reaction when you manage to change one. You see, core beliefs do not exist in isolation. Often, they feed into and reinforce one another. If one of your beliefs is that you are lazy and the other is that you are incompetent, then those beliefs will prop one another up. If, however, you manage to change the belief that you are lazy, you'll end up becoming more productive. By becoming more productive, you'll improve your performance and start doing better work. This will effectively dismantle your belief that you are incompetent because how could you be when you're killing it at work? Coupled with affirmations targeting your negative thoughts about your incompetence, this belief will soon collapse as well. This will keep happening with other negative beliefs you hold onto. Before you know it, pretty much all your beliefs will have completely changed, perhaps without you even realizing it.

Affirmations can be incredibly effective in changing your beliefs. This is actually why most people call them "affirmations" as opposed to "mantras" or some other term. The word "affirmation" means "affirming a belief" (Jarrels, 2021). The word "affirm" means to state something as a fact and to assert it. When you use affirmations regularly you end up changing your thoughts, mindset, and beliefs. You even end up changing your subconscious mind. This is a good thing because about 80% of your subconscious mind is guarded by negativity. This is all because of another cognitive bias we all have called the negativity bias. The negativity bias is your tendency to pay more attention to and ascribe more significance to negative thoughts, beliefs, and events. It's also your tendency to remember negative thoughts more than positive ones. Negativity bias originally used to be a survival tactic. It was meant to help you notice immediate threats in your vicinity, like a predator near the cave you are in, so that you can take action quickly, like by running away. It was also meant to help us remember potential threats and thus avoid them, like by making you vividly remember that that one plant you ate years ago got you violently sick, thereby giving you ample reason to stay away from it.

The problem with negativity bias is that you no longer live in the neolithic times. So, you don't face the same kinds of risks on a day to day basis. Yet the bias remains and causes you to focus on negative things explicitly, including your so-called negative traits. This puts you in a negative mindset and causes you to develop limiting beliefs, as you've seen, which take root in your subconscious. Affirmations uproot these beliefs from where they have become entrenched. They do so bit by bit, through repetition after repetition, until they start sinking in. Once they have, it doesn't take all that much more effort for them to turn into your new beliefs. That's not to say, affirmation will stop you from ever having any negative thoughts. Far from it. They will, however, prevent those thoughts from impacting you in the way that they used to and they will ensure that they pop into your mind far less often than they used to.

Ways to Incorporate Affirmations Into Your Life

We all live incredibly busy, even hectic lives, with a myriad of responsibilities. There's everything you have to do at work, commuting to the office, taking care of your family and then actually spending time with them, taking care of your own physical needs, cleaning up the house… With all that going, it is understandable that you feel a little or more than a little exhausted. It is even understandable that you have a tough time trying to schedule in your affirmations for the day. Tough, however, doesn't mean impossible, especially with something as necessary as affirmations. A great strategy to incorporate affirmations to your daily life is to make sure to do them at the same time every day. Most people try to pencil them in for the morning, right after they wake up, or at night, before they go to bed. Some people make them a part of their "getting ready" routine, repeating their affirmations to themselves as they are getting dressed or brushing their hair or putting on cologne.

These are all sound methods to adopt, so long as you know what your affirmations are going to be. Another method might be to physically schedule an alarm for yourself. This way, you can be sure you don't forget to repeat your affirmations to yourself on especially busy days. While you're doing this, you can also set up a 60 second long timer. You can repeat those affirmations over and over again, until those 60 seconds are up. When they are, you can turn off your alarm and get back to whatever it was you were doing, be it work, cooking dinner, or tackling another one of your many responsibilities.

Another great idea is to find songs that embody the messages you're trying to give to yourself through your affirmations and then to make a playlist of them. Then, you can listen to this playlist on a regular basis. You can play it when you're getting ready for the day, for instance, or on your commute back home from work.

Songs aren't the only tools you can use to reaffirm your affirmations. You can turn to books—like this one—movies, podcasts, and more as well. You can use any kind of media that you consume to your advantage in this regard and start making more conscious choices about them as a result. In the process, you can really fortify the positive beliefs and belief systems you're creating with your affirmations and thus, start manifesting the exact kind of life you want to live.

As you can see, there are many ways you can make your chosen affirmations a part of your everyday schedule. Repeating your affirmations to yourself doesn't have to be some great, time consuming exercise. Instead, it can be something you couple with other activities you have to do anyways. Likewise, the messages they give you can be strengthened through other things you do in your life, even activities that you'd be doing for fun and entertainment purposes. What all this means is that you really have no reason to forgo affirmations. Adopting them is fairly easy, so long as you show the tiniest bit of effort. Considering the immense impact that they can have in your life, it can be arguably said that they are well worth that effort, can it not?

Conclusion:

Your Mind Creates

How many times have you heard about how powerful the human mind is? How many amazing stories have you read about incredible people utterly transforming their lives? If you've made it to the end of this book, then that means you've at last begun your self-growth journey. Now, it is time to take those first real, major steps along your route and discover the hidden power your conscious and subconscious minds hold.

By now, you know that your mindset is if you want to achieve the success and well-being you desire. You understand that your beliefs and thoughts influence your reality and shape both your actions. They determine how you react to the various goings on around you too. Now, it is time to go further, to push yourself toward a deeper understanding of how you can use the full potential your mindset has to offer. Thought of in these terms, your brain can be considered an internal navigation system of sorts, one that guides you toward the life you desire. Once you understand the power of your subconscious mind, you can begin to use it as a compass pointing the way toward happiness, success, and abundance.

To begin this transformation is to recognize that you create your reality. Your mind is an incubator where thoughts and emotions take shape. They, in turn, shape the very fabric of your life and being. You decide which seeds to plant, meaning which thoughts to nurture, and which emotions to cultivate. Your mind is a greenhouse, and you are its gardener. If you want to have a lush greenhouse, then you have to choose which seeds to plant very wisely and then tend to them with love and care.

A key element in using the power of your mind is optimism. When you're able to see the positive side of situations, you become able to discover hidden opportunities in any situation you are in. This includes any challenges you face. Thus, you create a positive flow of energy that feeds your subconscious mind. Optimism becomes the sunshine that your greenhouse needs, nourishing the seeds that you've planted. But optimism alone is not enough. You must also learn to attract that which you desire into your life. This is where the law of attraction comes in. Your mind is a magnet. It attracts whatever it focuses on, as you've seen. If you focus your thoughts and emotions on what you don't want, then unfortunately that's what you'll attract. If, however, you focus on what you want to manifest, you'll attract the circumstances, people and opportunities that will lead you toward your goal toward yourself.

You have learned so much throughout the course of the *Optimism Mindset Bible*. You've gained some deep insights on the mindset, optimism, manifestation, and the many other personal growth tools at your disposal. Now it is time to put what you've learned into practice and use your mind to guide yourself toward the life you desire. You have the power to create the reality you want. What's more, you've already embarked on the path of manifestation, and at long last, it is time to bring to life everything you've dreamed of.

So, take a moment to imagine what you'd like your life to be like. Picture it down to the tiniest detail. Imagine what the work you love is like, what meaningful relationships you have, how vibrant you want your health to be, as well as the sheer abundance around you and inner peace you feel. This vision will become the starting point for your creation. Remember to engage in this exercise of imagination with passion and feeling, because your emotions ultimately amplify the power of your mind.

While you do this, keep the law of attraction at the back of your mind. Focus on the things you want, instead of the things you don't. Do not allow fear, self-doubt or any perceived limitations to drag you away from your vision. Be the keeper of your thoughts and stand firm in your confidence.

As you do this, rely on the tools you now know populate your toolkit. Remember that the 369 Method has taught how important repeating positive affirmations is and how it stimulates your subconscious to work in your favor. Incorporate this practice into your daily routine. Repeat your affirmations to yourself every day, with deep conviction. Tune into how the reality of what you are affirming feels, as if it was already an integral part of your life. Believe unconditionally in your ability to create the reality you desire.

Rely on positive psychology, which is a trusted companion for you in your personal growth journey. Learn to recognize your strengths, practice gratitude, and cultivate kindness. Make these habits a vital part of your being.

Always remember that your mind creates because you are an integral part of the creative energy of the universe. You have been gifted with an incredible brain that can connect with the vast power of the subconscious mind and translate your thoughts into concrete actions. When you realize that you're the creator of your reality, you become aware of your power. You have the power to choose the thoughts you feed, the words you speak, and the actions you take. These elements come together to create the energy that attracts your desires into your life. This is why you'll attract circumstances and people who support you in achieving your goals if you maintain a positive and optimistic mindset, if you believe in yourself and your abilities.

Another reason why your mind creates is that your subconscious is a storehouse of unlimited potential. You can access this resource through practices like self-hypnosis, visualization, and positive emotions. When you communicate what you wish to manifest to your subconscious mind, it starts working tirelessly to realize it. The subconscious knows no limits and has no concept of the impossible. It is a valuable ally that guides you toward success and abundance.

The power of your mind goes beyond the manifestation of material goods. It extends to creating the love, happiness and health you desire too. When you cultivate positive thoughts and focus on love and gratitude, you transform your inner reality and positively affect your physical and emotional well-being. Your mind is the bridge between your inner world and the outer world, and you have the power to shape both.

Now, dear reader, it is time to put all that you've learned into practice. Don't let these words be just a set of theoretical concepts, but turn them into concrete actions. Take the reins of your life into your hands and become the director of your own destiny. Keep a positive mindset, focus on your goals, and experience the magic of your mind's power. Remind yourself that change requires commitment and perseverance. Be patient with and kind toward yourself during this process, because every step forward counts as progress. Don't allow temporary obstacles or setbacks to discourage you. They are part of your growth journey, and every challenge overcome will make you stronger and more determined.

Your mind is an extraordinary gift, and by using it consciously as a guide leading you where you want to go, you can transform your life into a masterpiece of self-actualization and everlasting happiness. So, always remember that you're the captain of your ship. Do not allow anyone or anything to limit the power of your mind. Embrace your authenticity and be courageous in pursuing your dreams.

When confronted with obstacles, remember that you have the power to overcome them. Use your skills, determination and resilience to face challenges with confidence. Be flexible and adaptable, because change is inevitable and often brings with it unexpected opportunities. Never forget how important your connection with others is. Your creative mind is enriched through mutual support and inspiration. Share your knowledge, experiences and love with the world. When you get up, take others with you, because true success is collective.

At this point, dear reader, you've reached a crucial point in your journey. You have learned, you've absorbed, and you've experienced many things. Hence, it is finally time to take action. It is time to put all that you've learned into practice and create the life you deserve. In this way, you can make each day an opportunity to express your potential, to manifest the love, health, abundance and success you desire.

Your final chapter is just the beginning of a new adventure. Now, go forth and create your wonderful reality!

Love, Your Fellow Traveler

Affirmations

50 Affirmations on Couple Love

- ❖ I am worthy of a loving and healthy relationship.
- ❖ My partner and I support and cherish each other.
- ❖ Our love grows stronger every day.
- ❖ We communicate openly and honestly with each other.
- ❖ We are each other's best friend and confidant.
- ❖ Our relationship is built on trust and mutual respect.
- ❖ We make time for each other, no matter how busy our schedules are.
- ❖ We prioritize each other's happiness and well-being.
- ❖ Our love is unconditional and enduring.
- ❖ We are committed to building a lifetime of love together.
- ❖ Our love is a source of strength and inspiration for us both.
- ❖ We appreciate and value each other's unique qualities and strengths.

- We celebrate each other's successes and support each other through challenges.
- Our love is a safe and comforting haven in a sometimes harsh world.
- We are grateful for each other and for the love that we share.
- We choose each other every day.
- Our love is built on a foundation of mutual trust and understanding.
- We respect each other's boundaries and needs.
- We listen to each other with an open heart and mind.
- We communicate with kindness and compassion.
- We forgive each other when we make mistakes.
- We are patient and understanding with each other.
- We take care of each other's physical, emotional, and spiritual needs.
- We find joy and laughter in each other's company.
- We support each other's goals and dreams.
- We are better together than we are alone.
- We learn from each other and grow together.
- Our love is a partnership based on equality and shared responsibility.
- We are a team, and we work together to overcome obstacles.

- We make decisions together and respect each other's opinions.
- We appreciate each other's differences and learn from them.
- We are committed to keeping the spark of romance alive in our relationship.
- We show each other affection and tenderness every day.
- We never take each other for granted.
- We appreciate and express gratitude for the small things we do for each other.
- Our love is a refuge from the stresses of everyday life.
- We make time for fun and playful moments together.
- We enjoy trying new things and exploring the world together.
- We support each other's hobbies and interests.
- We respect and accept each other's flaws and imperfections.
- We always find a way to make up after an argument.
- We never go to bed angry with each other.
- We keep our promises and follow through on our commitments to each other.
- We are loyal and faithful to each other.

❖ We always make time to listen to each other's thoughts and feelings.

❖ We are attentive and present when we spend time together.

❖ We share our hopes and dreams for the future with each other.

❖ We are each other's rock in times of trouble.

❖ We share our worries and fears with each other and find solutions together.

❖ We always make time for a date night or a special occasion.

50 Love Affirmations for Single People

❖ I am deserving of love and companionship.

❖ I am open and receptive to love in all its forms.

❖ I radiate love and attract it effortlessly.

❖ I trust that love will come to me at the right time and in the right way.

❖ I am whole and complete within myself, and love will enhance my life even more.

- Love is a natural part of my life, and it flows to me with ease.

- I am grateful for the love that already exists in my life.

- I am worthy of a fulfilling and joyful relationship.

- I choose to focus on the positive aspects of love and relationships.

- I am ready to receive and give love in a healthy and supportive way.

- Love is abundant, and there is plenty for everyone, including me.

- I am confident and secure in myself, and this attracts love to me.

- I am open to learning and growing through my experiences with love.

- I trust that I will find someone who is a perfect match for me.

- I am open to exploring different types of love and relationships.

- I am deserving of respect, kindness, and affection from my partner.

- I am capable of loving deeply and fully.

- ❖ I am a magnet for love and positive energy.

- ❖ I am attracting the love I desire into my life right now.

- ❖ I am surrounded by love, and it fills me up.

- ❖ Love is a beautiful thing, and I am ready to experience it.

- ❖ I am open to receiving love in unexpected ways.

- ❖ I trust that the universe will bring me the love I need.

- ❖ I am worthy of a partner who respects and supports me.

- ❖ Love is an adventure, and I am excited to see where it takes me.

- ❖ I am open to the possibility of finding love online.

- ❖ I am grateful for the lessons I have learned through past relationships.

- ❖ I am confident in my ability to create a loving and healthy relationship.

- ❖ I am open to trying new things in order to find love.

- ❖ I am worthy of being loved for who I am.

- ❖ Love is a beautiful journey, and I am excited to be on it.

- ❖ I am attracting the love that aligns with my values and desires.

- ❖ I am worthy of being cherished and adored by my partner.

- ❖ I am confident in my ability to express my needs and boundaries in a relationship.

- ❖ Love is a powerful force, and it fills my life with joy and happiness.

- ❖ I am open to the idea of a long-distance relationship if it feels right.

- ❖ I am worthy of being with someone who makes me feel special and appreciated.

- ❖ Love is a journey, and I am enjoying every step of it.

- ❖ I trust that I will find someone who loves and accepts me unconditionally.

- ❖ I am open to the possibility of rekindling a past relationship if it feels right.

- ❖ I am grateful for the love that already exists in my life, including friendships and family.

- ❖ I am worthy of a partner who supports and encourages me to pursue my dreams.

- ❖ I am confident in my ability to communicate effectively in a relationship.

- ❖ Love is a beautiful thing, and I am excited to experience it with someone special.

- ❖ I am open to meeting new people and exploring new possibilities.

- ❖ I am attracting the love that brings out the best in me.

- ❖ I am worthy of a partner who shares my values and beliefs.

- ❖ I am open to the idea of a non-traditional relationship if it feels right.

- ❖ Love is a gift, and I am grateful for every moment of it.

- ❖ I am open to taking the time necessary to find the right partner for me.

50 Affirmations to Attract Wealth and Abundance

- ❖ I am learning and growing to improve my finances.

- I am always finding Money comes to me easily and effortlessly.

- I am deserving of financial abundance.

- I am grateful for the wealth that is flowing into my life.

- The universe is constantly providing me with opportunities to grow my wealth.

- My bank account is constantly increasing.

- I am open and receptive to all forms of abundance.

- I have a positive relationship with money.

- I am attracting financial opportunities into my life.

- I am a magnet for prosperity and abundance.

- I have a millionaire mindset.

- Wealth flows into my life with ease and grace.

- I am open to receiving wealth in all areas of my life.

- I have the power to create wealth and abundance.

- I am worthy of receiving abundant wealth.

- I am rich in love, health, and wealth.

- My bank account is always growing.

- ❖ My financial abundance is increasing every day.
- ❖ I am financially free and independent.
- ❖ I am always surrounded by abundance.
- ❖ I attract wealth and prosperity effortlessly.
- ❖ I am grateful for the abundance that surrounds me.
- ❖ I attract wealth into my life by living in alignment with my purpose.
- ❖ Money comes to me in unexpected ways.
- ❖ I am open and receptive to receiving money.
- ❖ I am grateful for the wealth that I have and the wealth that is coming to me.
- ❖ I am constantly attracting financial opportunities.
- ❖ My income is constantly increasing.
- ❖ I am financially secure and stable.
- ❖ I am attracting abundance in every area of my life.
- ❖ I am a powerful creator of my financial destiny.
- ❖ I am capable of achieving financial freedom.
- ❖ I am worthy of having an abundant life.

- Wealth and prosperity are my birthright.
- I am always in the right place at the right time to receive financial abundance.
- I am aligned with the energy of abundance.
- I am surrounded by abundance and prosperity.
- I am grateful for the wealth that is flowing into my life.
- I am a magnet for success and abundance.
- I am open to receiving wealth from multiple sources.
- I am financially abundant and wealthy.
- I am constantly attracting new streams of income.
- I am open and receptive to receiving financial abundance.
- My bank account is always overflowing with money.
- I am grateful for the abundance that I have and the abundance that is coming to me.
- I am attracting wealth and success into my life effortlessly.
- I am living a life of abundance and prosperity.
- I am a money magnet.

- I am attracting financial freedom into my life.
- I am attracting wealth in every area of my life.

50 Affirmations for Money and Success

- Money flows to me easily and effortlessly.
- I am a money magnet and attract abundance into my life.
- Success comes naturally to me.
- I deserve abundance and prosperity.
- I am worthy of great wealth and success.
- I have a positive and prosperous mindset.
- Opportunities to earn money come to me easily and frequently.
- I am open to receiving abundance from multiple sources.
- I am grateful for the abundance in my life.
- I am capable of achieving financial freedom.
- I am financially abundant and secure.

- ❖ I am prosperous in every aspect of my life.

- ❖ Money is just energy, and I attract positive energy.

- ❖ I have everything I need to be successful.

- ❖ I am confident in my ability to create wealth and abundance.

- ❖ My mind is focused on achieving financial success.

- ❖ I am surrounded by people who support my success and growth.

- ❖ I am constantly new and creative ways to make money.

- ❖ I am constantly attracting new opportunities for success and prosperity.

- ❖ I am a natural at creating wealth and success.

- ❖ My wealth and success inspire others to achieve greatness.

- ❖ I am a master at managing my finances.

- ❖ I am constantly improving my financial literacy.

- ❖ I am deserving of all the wealth and success I achieve.

- ❖ I am grateful for the financial abundance in my life.

- ❖ I am worthy of a life filled with financial abundance.

- ❖ I am living my dream life of abundance and success.
- ❖ I am constantly attracting new and exciting opportunities for wealth and success.
- ❖ I am always focused on achieving my financial goals.
- ❖ I am a successful entrepreneur who creates wealth and abundance.
- ❖ I am confident in my ability to achieve financial freedom.
- ❖ I am worthy of receiving wealth and success into my life.
- ❖ I am attracting success and prosperity into my life every day.
- ❖ My mind is always focused on abundance and prosperity.
- ❖ I am worthy of living a life of luxury and abundance.
- ❖ I am grateful for the financial freedom I have achieved.
- ❖ I am constantly attracting new and exciting business opportunities.
- ❖ I am surrounded by abundance and prosperity.
- ❖ I am a successful business owner who creates wealth and prosperity.

- ❖ I am worthy of a life filled with financial abundance and success.

- ❖ I am always attracting abundance and prosperity into my life.

- ❖ I am constantly finding new ways to increase my wealth and success.

- ❖ I am attracting abundance into every aspect of my life.

- ❖ I am grateful for the financial abundance that surrounds me.

- ❖ I am worthy of all the success and abundance I achieve.

- ❖ I am a magnet for financial prosperity.

- ❖ I am constantly attracting new opportunities for success and wealth.

- ❖ I am deserving of financial abundance in my life.

- ❖ I am living my dream life of financial abundance and success.

- ❖ I am attracting wealth and success effortlessly and naturally.

Image References

- CDD20. (2020, May 4). *Cartoon Heart*. [Image]. Pixabay. https://pixabay.com/illustrations/cartoon-painting-fantasy-5123462/
- CDD20. (2020, March 8). *Creativity*. [Image]. Pixabay. https://pixabay.com/illustrations/creativity-thinking-painting-4912657/
- CDD20. (2016, February 8). *Growth*. [Image]. Pixabay. https://pixabay.com/illustrations/fairy-tale-night-flower-girl-star-1182696/
- CDD20. (2020, December 20). *Human Soul*. [Image]. Pixabay. https://pixabay.com/illustrations/human-soul-universe-stars-starry-5831238/
- CDD20. (2020, June 7). *Stars*. [Image]. Pixabay. https://pixabay.com/illustrations/caricature-painting-fantasy-5268739/
- CDD20. (2020, May 4). *The Universe*. [Image]. Pixabay. https://pixabay.com/illustrations/cartoon-painting-universe-5124000/
- CDD20. (2020, December 20). *Touch Hands*. [Image]. Pixabay. https://pixabay.com/illustrations/touch-hands-universe-space-stars-5831241/
- CDD20. (2020, May 11). *Universe Hand*. [Image]. Pixabay. https://pixabay.com/illustrations/handshake-imagination-fairy-tale-5153649/
- CDD20. (2020, December 27). Girl Reach Universe. [Image]. Pixabay. https://pixabay.com/illustrations/girl-moon-universe-reach-catch-5831275/
- Gerd Altmann. (2017, July 18). Starry Sky Meditation. [Image]. Pixabay. https://pixabay.com/illustrations/starry-sky-meditation-cross-legged-2515489/

www.ingramcontent.com/pod-product-compliance
Lightning Source LLC
Chambersburg PA
CBHW072154070526
44585CB00015B/1131